EMU RACING AND RECORD CHASING

EMU
RACING

RECORD
CHASING

Tom Davies

Matador
9 Priory Business Park,
Wistow Road, Kibworth Beauchamp,
Leicestershire. LE8 0RX
Tel: 0116 279 2299
Email: books@troubador.co.uk
Web: www.troubador.co.uk/matador
Twitter: @matadorbooks

ISBN 978 1789016 949

British Library Cataloguing in Publication Data.
A catalogue record for this book is available from the British Library.

Printed by TJ International, Padstow, Cornwall
Typeset in 11pt Minio Pro by Troubador Publishing Ltd, Leicester, UK

Matador is an imprint of Troubador Publishing Ltd

For Mum, Dad and Anna

CONTENTS

MAPS

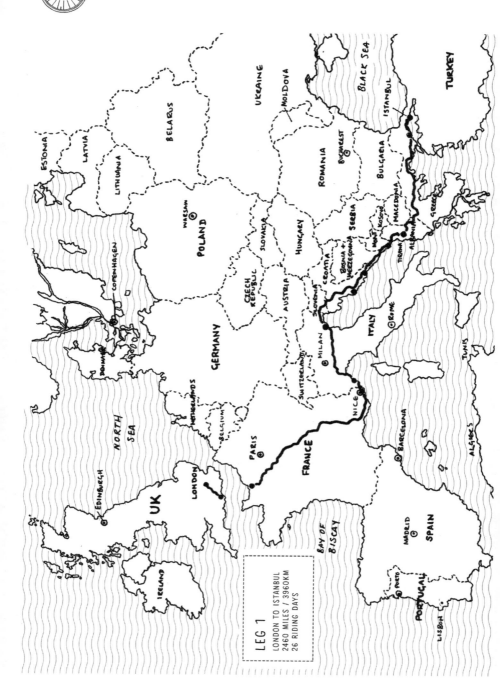

LEG 1

LONDON TO ISTANBUL
2460 MILES / 3960KM
26 RIDING DAYS

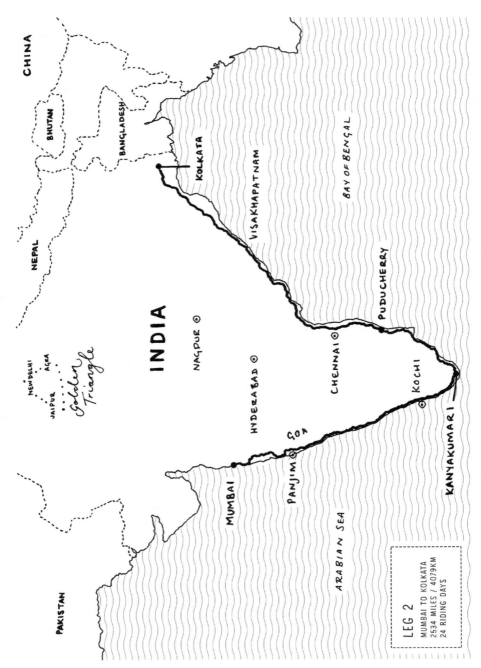

LEG 2
MUMBAI TO KOLKATA
2534 MILES / 4079KM
24 RIDING DAYS

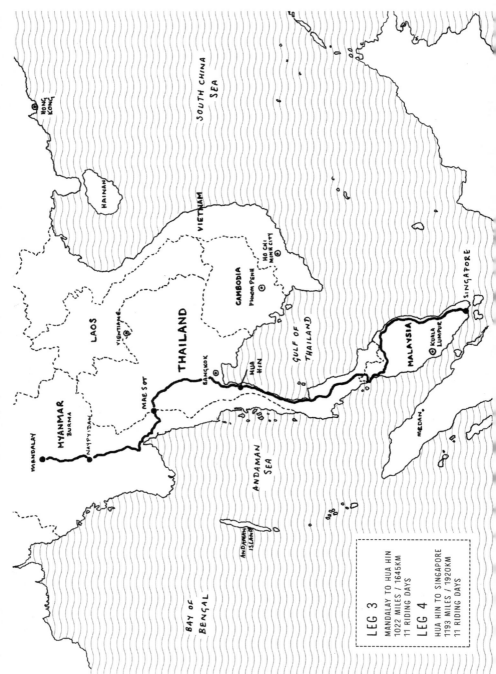

LEG 3
MANDALAY TO HUA HIN
1022 MILES / 1645KM
11 RIDING DAYS

LEG 4
HUA HIN TO SINGAPORE
1193 MILES / 1920KM
11 RIDING DAYS

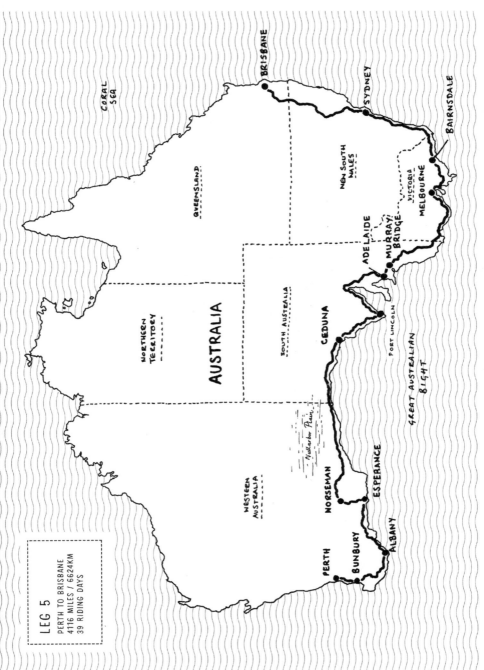

LEG 5

PERTH TO BRISBANE
4116 MILES / 6624KM
39 RIDING DAYS

CORAL SEA

BRISBANE

SYDNEY

BAIRNSDALE

QUEENSLAND

NEW SOUTH WALES

VICTORIA

MELBOURNE

ADELAIDE

MURRAY BRIDGE

NORTHERN TERRITORY

AUSTRALIA

SOUTH AUSTRALIA

CEDUNA

PORT LINCOLN

GREAT AUSTRALIAN BIGHT

WESTERN AUSTRALIA

Nullarbor Plain

NORSEMAN

ESPERANCE

ALBANY

PERTH

BUNBURY

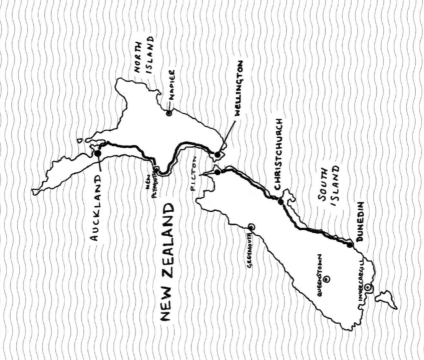

NORTH
ISLAND

NAPIER

WELLINGTON

CHRISTCHURCH

SOUTH
ISLAND

AUCKLAND

NEW
PLYMOUTH

PICTON

NEW ZEALAND

DUNEDIN

GREYMOUTH

QUEENSTOWN

INVERCARGILL

TASMAN SEA

LEG 6

DUNEDIN TO AUCKLAND
942 MILES / 1516KM
9 RIDING DAYS

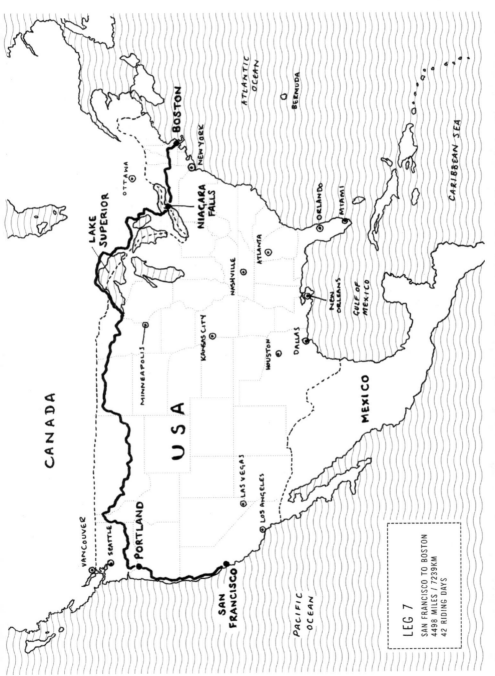

LEG 7

SAN FRANCISCO TO BOSTON
4498 MILES / 7239KM
42 RIDING DAYS

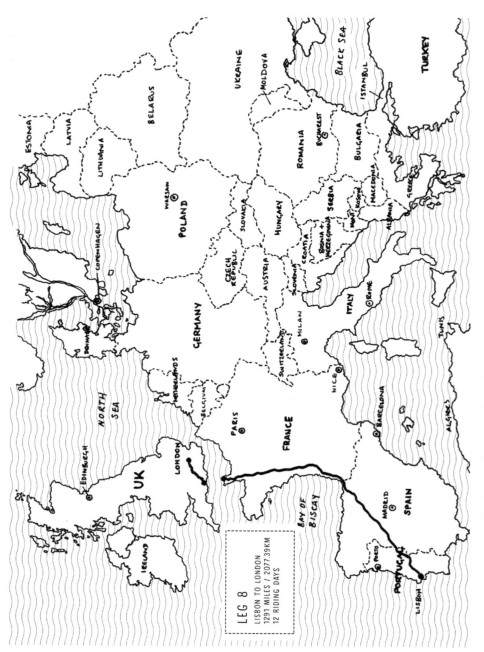

LEG 8

LISBON TO LONDON
1291 MILES / 2077.39KM
12 RIDING DAYS

INTRODUCTION

When I was 19, I became the youngest person to cycle around the world. Throughout this 18,000-mile ride around the planet, I wrote a blog every day. A number of people asked me to follow up with a book, suggesting that, along with some very crisp tan lines, I must have come back with a story worth reading. Whether or not that is true remains to be seen, but this is that book.

It took me a long time to figure out what I wanted to say and how I wanted to say it, but, after scrapping my first few attempts, I have finally come up with something that I'm happy with. I may touch on a few delicate topics and I may use a few swear words, but I promise not to go too far.

I have aimed to put a different spin on my account compared to similar books that are out there. Whilst this is fundamentally about my journey around the world, I did not want it to be a generic summary of what happened every day. My blog did a good job of representing my day-to-day frustrations, so I have done my best to avoid repeating myself. My blog is still available (*www.tomdaviesrtw.com/blog/*), so if that would interest you, please feel free to read it.

Something I have always been a big advocate of – particularly in regard to this trip – is authenticity. My intention is not to sell you a lie, and tell a story of the guy who exceeded expectations with ease and smiled the whole way. I was honest in my blog, and I wanted to be honest here. What follows is a look at the world from a bicycle saddle and I have kept it as genuine and unsanitised as possible. I hope it's interesting, I hope it makes you laugh and I hope it gives you an idea of why I did what I did.

Disclaimer: My ride around the world put me under considerable stress and I often saw the worst of the countries I visited. So, whilst I hope they are fairly amusing, my thoughts on the places I went to should not be taken too seriously. If you believe me to be mistaken, it's very likely that I am, so please just ignore any or all of the assumptions I have made.

The truth is, I was just a normal adolescent afraid of growing up when I set off, and I was still deeply insecure and immature when I first started this book. It took me a long time to digest the experience, and, although not ideal, the three-year delay was necessary. Anyway, this is my story; I hope it's worth the wait.

WHY DID I DO IT?

It's a seemingly innocent question, one that I get asked more than any other, and yet it's still the one I find hardest to answer. I get many variations of it: "Why cycle around the world?", "Why not do something normal?", "Why did you want to do it?", and, my personal favourite, "Why not just drive a fucking car?". This last one came whilst I was buying a bacon sandwich in an Australian roadhouse, 100 kilometres away from the next building.

I have spoken to a couple of people who know what they are talking about when it comes to writing books, and they told me to put the answer to this question at the beginning. Apparently, it tells people what they want to know, and it introduces the reader to who I am.

Despite this advice, I am slightly against the idea. Firstly, I find it very difficult to put my answer into words. Secondly, I hope that, throughout this book, I will be able to provide some justification for doing what I did. I hope that, by the time you finish reading, you will already have an idea of the answer and won't think I'm completely insane. If not, I will answer the question at the end as best I can. Lastly, I enjoy doing things unconventionally, so if that's one more way that I can flip things around, then all the better.

For now, I shall provide a partially honest (and probably unsatisfying) answer: I don't know why. I forced myself through injury, illness, wind, rain, heat, sleet and snow. In many ways, it was a pretty stupid thing to do.

THE FINAL ITINERARY

My route – as was the case with many of the plans I made – changed on numerous occasions leading up to, and during, my trip. Even when I reached North America, two-thirds of the way round, I was still making fairly major alterations to the route I was going to take. So, to keep confusion to a minimum, I think it's a good idea if I fill you in on the final route and schedule I ended up taking, just so that you have an idea of what's going on. I have included maps at the start of this book (wonderfully drawn by Hannah Rummery), indicating the actual routes taken, so feel free to just look at those if you're not interested in the intricacies of the trip.

I started at my home in London, and the first day was a ride down to Portsmouth, where I boarded an overnight ferry to Caen (France). Over the next five days, I headed through the middle of France in the general direction of Monaco. My dad joined me in a car halfway through Day 7, and he left towards the end of Day 9, after having accompanied me along the south coast of France. I then spent the next 17 days riding onwards to Istanbul – via the Adriatic coast.

I flew to Mumbai from Istanbul, and rode down the west

coast and up the east coast of India until I reached Kolkata after a total of 24 days.

Next, I took another flight to Mandalay in Burma (now Myanmar). It took me 10 days to ride from Mandalay to Hua Hin (just south of Bangkok), where I met my whole family, who had come out for my sister Anna's 18th birthday. I had five days off there, then had another 10 days riding to Singapore via Malaysia, before flying on to Australia.

I followed the coast of Australia from Perth all the way to Brisbane (4,200 miles) over the next 42 days. Just after Adelaide, I was joined for a seven-day stretch by Ray, Steve and Richard (my dad's uncle and cousins), until Bairnsdale on the other side of Melbourne.

My dad flew out to drive the New Zealand leg with me. I started in Dunedin and finished in Auckland. It took 10 days, but one of those was spent crossing between the South and North Islands. Dad then flew back to London, and I headed on to San Francisco.

San Francisco to Boston was 4,500 miles, and it took me 42 days. I began by riding up the coast of California, before cutting inland in Oregon. I continued north via Portland, and into Washington state. I then headed east through the northern states, until I reached Lake Superior in Minnesota. At this point, I followed the lake's north shore into Canada. I took a fairly direct route to Niagara Falls, where I re-entered the US. From there it was a relatively straight line to Boston.

I started my final leg in Lisbon, and it took me 12 days to arrive back in London. I was joined by Dad, my cousin Henry and my godfather Nige on my final evening in northern Spain. They stayed with me for the remaining six days through France.

The whole trip took 205 days, 174 of which were spent riding. My target before setting off had been to do it in 180 days' riding, as that worked out at an average of 100 miles a day. The final mileage was 18,046 (approximately 29,000 kilometres) give or take a couple. It was over 18,000 miles, which is what mattered – something I'll explain in the next chapter.

So, over the course of the trip, I had 31 'rest' days, compared to 174 riding days. Saying it like that equates to having a day off every six or seven days, which sounds a bit excessive. However, many of them were either logistically necessary because of flights, or because I was staying with friends or family. It would have been a bit rude if I had just carried on cycling when others had made a huge effort to come and see, or look after me.

Whilst I was keen to maintain a respectable speed, my ride around the world was not a race. I wanted to challenge myself, but, equally, I did not want to go all the way around the world and miss everything. It was up to me to find my own balance between pushing myself and experiencing the places I went to. Thankfully, being a fairly rubbish tourist, these two goals rarely conflicted with each other. I was mostly content just glimpsing the places I visited, and, in reality, I spent the majority of my time riding through large, open spaces, so there wasn't always much call for sightseeing. It was nice to have a little bit of down time whenever I reached an airport though.

On these occasions, I was often met by someone from my family in order to swap my kit over, provide me with essential bike parts and help me navigate whatever city I found myself in. For example, the change from European winter to the heat of India was particularly dramatic, and required a whole new wardrobe.

My first rest day came in Diano Marina (Italy) after nine days' riding. Having just started the trip, my body was not yet accustomed to the workload, and knee pain was becoming a genuine issue. I needed to stop to give my knee a chance to recover. As it happened, taking that day off, whilst relaxing, was one of the worst things I could have done. My injured knee didn't improve, I got food poisoning and I was therefore forced into another day off the bike. Two weeks later, as a consequence of the delay, I ran into a blizzard in Greece, which put me even further behind schedule.

I had crossed into Italy a few hours before arriving in Diano Marina, so, despite having a couple of problems, I was feeling optimistic. Italy is incredible; ask someone to describe it, and they will conjure images of rolling Tuscan hills, iconic Venetian waterways and bustling Roman piazzas. I was looking forward to what the country held, and that is without even mentioning the food.

Italy is famed for its food, and rightly so. Second only to France in my personal preferences, this was not a country I expected to poison me. Nevertheless, I woke up at 1am the morning after my rest day, having to rush to the toilet to be sick. This continued every hour until 6am, by which time I had finally stopped trying to get back to sleep and resigned myself to the fact that I would not be riding my bike that day. I slumped against the toilet bowl and kept being sick for most of the morning. By the time dinner came around, I asked for a bowl of plain pasta and forced myself to eat something. When I set off riding the next day, I was behind schedule and in a much worse condition than when I had stopped two days earlier. Not a very restful couple of days.

I met my dad when I got to Istanbul. He had brought almost an entire suitcase of different kit and bike parts. Once he had emptied it, I refilled it with all the things I no longer needed – a lot of cold- and wet-weather gear. We spent one day sorting out what kit we thought I would need and preparing the bike for a flight. This involved dismantling and packing it in a bike box. The following day was spent doing touristy things around the city. The Spice Bazaar is my recommended attraction.

I flew out the next day, and then had two days in Mumbai to acclimatise. Not only was it fascinating to be shown around the city and introduced to the culture, it was also absolutely essential. Had I gone off riding straight away without an introduction to the country, I would have come severely unstuck.

The four-day changeover from Kolkata to Mandalay followed a similar pattern with the same necessities. Hua Hin (Thailand) was a different story. I wasn't flying anywhere, and my parents and Anna had come out to see me for her 18th birthday. I had been away for a couple of months by this point, and it was purely a rest, nothing more. I ate copious amounts of food, and managed to put on a noticeable amount of weight in those five days.

The Singapore changeover followed the same principles and practical logistics as Istanbul and Kolkata (as did Auckland to San Francisco and Boston to Lisbon, which came later). My only other rest days came in Australia and New Zealand. The first was in Adelaide, to stay with friends, and then in Bairnsdale and Sydney, where each time I was staying with family.

The changeover from Brisbane to Dunedin (New Zealand) only lasted one day. There wasn't a big cultural difference to get used to, and there was no real point in wasting any time, so I started riding the day after I flew in.

My crossing from the South to the North Island of New Zealand also took a whole day, which was largely due to an unnecessary ferry delay – thanks Interislander Ferries.

The thing about many of these rest days was that they often weren't very restful. In terms of physical recovery, most of the rest days did help. The continental changeovers provided enough respite and generally benefitted my legs. However, each time I took a single day off, I would restart feeling just as tired. I had a two-month stretch from Perth to Auckland without consecutive days off, and when I got back on the bike in San Francisco after three days off, my body felt noticeably fresher. (In truth, it was actually more like four days because I crossed the International Date Line – something that really messed with my head at the time. Somehow, I landed in California before I set off from New Zealand.)

Mentally, things were a bit different. I was constantly stressed. Even if I tried to put things out of my mind, I could never completely switch off. I managed to relax a bit in Perth, Bairnsdale and Sydney, and for a couple of days in Hua Hin, but other than that I always felt as if I were on a knife-edge. I tried to remain focused on the task, as I was wary of letting myself get complacent.

I felt most stressed in Mandalay and Lisbon. In both cities, I spent my time rushing around sorting final details for the upcoming ride. In Mandalay, it was trying to work around the lack of any accurate maps, whereas, in Lisbon, it was fixing last-minute bike issues.

Lisbon was slightly different because much of my stress was self-inflicted. In Burma, I was mainly panicking about matters out of my control. There was so much I didn't know about the country, and I couldn't help but worry about things such as accommodation. In Lisbon, I arrived from Boston, where I had mistakenly allowed my brain to go to sleep. I had just finished 42 consecutive days' riding across North America, and I mentally shut down when I reached the end of that leg. When the time came to prepare for another fortnight of riding, I had lost most of my composure. Mum and Anna were waiting for me in Lisbon, and, although it was great to see them, I don't think they were overly grateful for the stress I brought with me.

The main problem arose when trying to fit a new chain to my bike. Although I knew what I had to do, I lacked the necessary tools. The next couple of hours were spent trying to find a bike shop and then explain, in my non-existent Portuguese, what needed to be done. It worked out in the end, but I think I nearly had an anxiety attack in the interim.

All in all, I would say that roughly 10 of the 31 rest days were actually mentally restful, and still fewer than 20 actively benefitted me physically. But never mind, rest is overrated anyway.

THE RECORD

The route I chose to take was decided based on a number of factors, and it was ultimately shaped by the guidelines drawn up by Guinness World Records (GWR).

Early on, I was disappointed by GWR when it said that it no longer officiates 'youngest person' records. I believe (at the time of writing this) that I am the youngest person to cycle around the world, but it is unofficial. I am happy to concede that someone else could have beaten my benchmark, but I have claimed to be the youngest for a while now, and no one has yet come forwards to suggest otherwise. In essence, I do not have a certificate of proof, but I'm fairly certain that I am currently the youngest person to have completed the task.

(October 2018 side note: I know of two guys – Jimmy Ashby and Charlie Condell – who are currently on track to break my record. I'm hoping that this book will be published before either of them finish, but please cut me some slack if it's not – I underestimated how long it would take to write!)

Despite this lack of official verification, I wanted to do the trip according to the guidelines GWR sets out. I wanted to know that I had completed the challenge to the standards it has set. For anybody wondering, I believe its reason for no longer endorsing 'youngest person' records is to discourage children taking on dangerous tasks, and to discourage overly pushy parents. I understand its stance, but it was irritating given that I was taking on the challenge regardless.

In hindsight, it became a blessing in disguise. It meant that I wasn't required to collect witness statements everywhere I went, which would have been a huge hassle. (I have other proof of what I did in case anybody thinks I may have exploited this loophole!)

Due to the lack of a 'youngest person to cycle around the world' record, I based my trip on the parameters governing a 'fastest circumnavigation by bike' attempt. There are a few rules that have to be adhered to for an official record; the key ones regarding the route are as follows:

1. THE JOURNEY SHOULD BE CONTINUAL AND IN ONE DIRECTION.
   In my case, this was east, and it essentially meant I had to choose between different potential routes; for example, North America or South America, Europe or Africa. I went for the northern route in both cases.

2. YOU MUST PASS THROUGH TWO APPROXIMATE ANTIPODAL POINTS (OPPOSITE POINTS ON THE GLOBE).
   The common ones to use are Wellington (New Zealand) and slightly north of Madrid (Spain). These worked for me.

3. THE START AND FINISH POINTS MUST BE THE SAME.
   In my case, my house in London.

4. THE TOTAL DISTANCE TRAVELLED (BY PLANE, BOAT, BIKE OR ANYTHING ELSE) MUST EXCEED THE LENGTH OF THE EQUATOR – 24,900 MILES (40,075 KILOMETRES). THE TOTAL DISTANCE TRAVELLED BY BIKE MUST EXCEED 18,000 MILES (28,970 KILOMETRES).
   This is the rule I wanted to be really hot on: 18,000 miles.

The planning for the route began by getting a rough idea of what other people had done. Along with that, the weather I would encounter was one of the main deciding factors. This was predicted based on the fact that I had to set off in January. I needed to plan, work and train beforehand (but after finishing school), and also had to be back in time to start university in September. In addition to the weather, the political situation at the time also had to be considered. Certain countries in the Middle East and Africa were struck off the list from the start. I had no intention of flirting with that kind of danger.

My parents and I, therefore, looked at where we could fit the necessary miles into the countries that remained an option. We were left with something that roughly resembled the final route. Cambodia and Vietnam were in the original plan, but that part of the route got changed for logistical reasons to tie in with my family's visit to Thailand in April.

Iran was also in my initial itinerary, but was removed on the basis that they would only grant me a visa if I had a permanent escort. I wasn't willing to do that. I have heard wonderful things about Iran, so this was a shame. I'd still love to go there some day. Georgia, Armenia and Azerbaijan were considered instead, but logistical issues complicated these options as well. Once those countries were out of the picture, I decided to remove the majority of Turkey. Other than Istanbul, I was not overly excited about riding through Turkey in winter. Retrospectively, I am glad I made that decision; I don't think that braving the winter weather for a further two weeks would have offered any benefit.

Removing the Middle Eastern portion left a large gap and a lot of miles that needed to be catered for. What remained was a reasonably select route, which then had to be altered further to give me the necessary 18,000 miles. For instance, riding down and up both coasts of India rather than going straight across, and continuing up the west coast of Australia to Brisbane rather than stopping in Sydney. It also gave me a reason to head into Canada during my North American leg.

Seven years prior to my trip, Mark Beaumont revolutionised cycling around the world. He was the first person to *race* it, and he set his target at 100 miles a day. This record has since been smashed several times (most recently by Beaumont himself), but he set the initial benchmark. It was after planning my route that I chose 100 miles as my daily target. I wanted to see and experience the world I was riding around, but I wanted to do it relatively fast at the same time. It was all about striking a balance between speed and experiences. Cycling 100 miles a day was my happy medium. It was a target that I felt would push me but not restrict me. Furthermore, 100 miles is a nice round number, which made planning ahead much easier.

As a side note, I jump around between miles and kilometres quite a lot in this book. I generally use kilometres, but I had a 100-mile daily target and an 18,000-mile finish target – hence, I often use both. I apologise for any confusion that may cause. Here is a handy conversion table of key values in case you ever get stuck:

HANDY CONVERSION TABLE

Miles	Kilometres
25	40
50	80
100	160
124	200
18,000	28,968

THE BIKE

Considering how crucial it was to the trip, it's probably about time that I mentioned the bike. The whole thing would have taken significantly longer had I not had it.

I used a Condor Fratello, a steel-framed road bike (and a bloody gorgeous one at that). Condor is a bike shop based in London, which has its handmade frames built over in Italy. Julian and Angel were the two guys who had the most input on putting my bike together, but I owe huge thanks to the whole team there, particularly Jaz and Mindy. They were always on hand to offer support throughout the whole trip.

To accompany the frame, I had a Condor Race wheelset – 32 spokes each – with Shimano Ultegra hubs; and I used Continental Gatorskin tyres – 28 millimetres or 32 millimetres, depending on where I was. The groupset was Shimano Ultegra 11-speed (excluding brakes), with a compact chainset (50–34) and 12–32 on the back. I chose Deda handlebars and stem, Shimano XT pedals and a Brooks Cambium C17 saddle. The brakes were TRP rim brakes to allow for more tyre clearance. The pannier rack, which was bought after the bike, was a Tubus titanium one. The whole thing weighed in at around 10–11 kilogrammes, but was pushed up to around 30 kilogrammes when fully loaded.

I realise these details will mean nothing to a lot of people, so in the interest of keeping things engaging, I shall stop there. I have included a picture (see over page) aimed at helping some of you if I ever mention bike-related things.

Something also worth mentioning at this stage is my Garmin, which I used for navigation. I am often asked how I dealt with that, and whether I used hard-copy maps. Aside from Burma – where digital maps were largely inaccurate – I relied on my Garmin Edge 1000 or Google Maps on my phone.

Navigation was rarely an issue. When riding across certain countries, there was often only one road to take. Out in the middle of Australia, I would wake up, and could either go right or left; one of those being the direction I had already come from. It was hard to go wrong in that situation.

Europe has a lot more roads than other places, so I was heavily reliant on my GPS whilst there. My dad would plan the routes (not a small task), and then I would upload them to my Garmin from wherever I happened to be.

Lastly, I also had a bike box for sending my bike on a plane. Using it was simple enough, but getting it to and from where I needed it to be was a logistical nightmare. In India, Australia and the US, it travelled across country by train, so it probably had an easier time of it than I did. The transport of my bike box was organised by Fereshte (India), Steve Elsworthy (Australia) and then Alison Davis (the US), after they had all let me stay with them during my time in their respective cities.

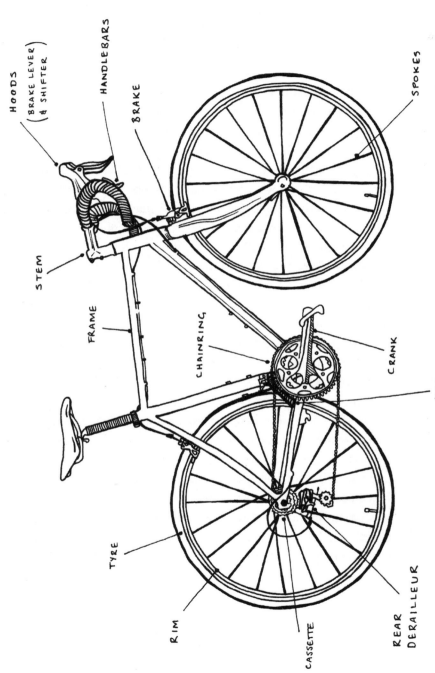

HOODS
(BRAKE LEVER & SHIFTER)

HANDLEBARS

BRAKE

SPOKES

STEM

FRAME

CHAINRING

CRANK

FRONT DERAILLEUR

TYRE

RIM

CASSETTE

REAR DERAILLEUR

BIKE MAINTENANCE

Before leaving, I think most people assumed that I was pretty handy when it came to bike maintenance. Regrettably, this was not the case. I got by on luck, the generosity of others and optimistic improvisation.

For every flight, I would have to take my bike apart and then put it back together at the other end. Theoretically, this isn't challenging, but it often turned out to be an extremely stressful experience. I have already alluded to the rush around Lisbon, but that wasn't the only time I struggled. In Mumbai, I had to build my bike in an unlit garage. Things became particularly difficult when a couple of screws went walkabout, and I was forced to improvise with some cable ties instead. It also required a little more effort than normal in Mandalay; I had Dad to help me, but doing it outside in 40°C made for a very sweaty affair.

There were inevitably a few other moments when my bike required attention, but, over the whole trip, I was actually very lucky when it came to mechanical issues. My overall statistics finished at 10 punctures, one snapped gear cable, one cracked wheel rim and seven broken spokes. I also wore out a bottom bracket, but that was changed by someone more competent than me.

Ten punctures over the course of 18,000 miles is really good going, especially taking into account the load I was carrying and the roads I was riding on. The first of these came in Albania, after 1,900 miles. Up to this point, there was genuinely a part of me that believed I would be able to go the whole way without a single one – although that was obviously a ridiculous fantasy. On this occasion, I was forced towards a very big pothole by a completely unaware driver, and – despite my best attempts to bunny-hop over it – caught my back wheel. I should stress that bunny-hopping a 30-kilogramme bike is neither easy nor advisable. In fairness to myself, avoiding both the swerving vehicle and the crater in the road was a near impossible task.

Fixing the subsequent puncture apparently proved extremely exciting for the locals, one of whom, a *slightly overweight* woman, proceeded to go and fetch a plastic chair, which she placed 10 metres away from me. She then sat down and watched me fix my puncture, without uttering a word, or even offering a smile for that matter.

The second puncture came on my first day in India – this time, it was completely my fault. I was descending a very broken road when I realised I was heading straight for another large hole. I made the split-second decision that braking and going around it would take too long; so, once again, I attempted to jump over it, and, once again, I failed.

Mercifully (and surprisingly), that was not a theme that continued throughout the rest of India. It wasn't until my penultimate day in the country that I suffered another puncture. The next one after that came in Thailand, and then in Australia, at which point I got two, one immediately after the other, because I had failed to remove the offending piece of metal from my tyre.

The remaining punctures all came in the US, and three out of those four happened on the same day. For anyone wondering, I changed my tyres every 3,000 miles or so (give or take a few hundred) to minimise the chances of completely wearing a set out.

The snapped gear cable happened in Thailand, 90 kilometres before the end of Leg 3. When this happens, the rear derailleur moves to the bottom of the cassette, essentially leaving you stuck in the hardest gear on your bike. If you happen to be a competent mechanic, it is possible to remedy this slightly and move the derailleur into a more comfortable gear. You still can't change gear, but it will mean you can ride efficiently until you manage to replace the broken cable. Unfortunately, my skills leaned towards incompetence, so, after failing to find an open bike shop in the next town, I decided that I would have to ride the remainder of the day grinding a big gear.

I had done about 5,500 miles without changing gear cables up to that point, so, in a sense, I had it coming. To be perfectly honest, it happened at a very convenient time, as I was able to get it fixed whilst I had five scheduled days off with my family in Hua Hin.

The broken spokes were the real pain in the arse. The first broke in Australia, in the middle of nowhere, the day before heading across the Nullarbor Plain. I heard a *twang*, and at first I thought something had flicked up and hit my frame. Without stopping, I checked my brakes and gears to make sure everything was still functioning, but then carried on. After another five minutes or so, I looked down and noticed that my rear wheel was wobbling all over the place. Realising what had happened, I pulled over and swore a lot. After a few minutes of panic, I ended up watching a YouTube video (many thanks to

GCN for that) on my phone, to guide me through the repair process. Pretty incredible (and fortunate) that I was able to do that in the middle of the Aussie Outback, miles from anywhere.

I eventually got it fixed, but not without a few difficulties. If you have no interest in bike-related talk, it may be worth skipping the rest of this paragraph. Thankfully, the spoke had broken on the non-drive side. I would have been really stuck if that had not been the case, as I don't think there was a chain whip anywhere other than 100 miles back the way I had come. This did not mean the cassette posed no problems though; I had a 32-tooth sprocket on the back, so even threading a spoke through the opposite side of the hub was impossible without bending it. I am no expert, but even I was fairly certain that bending a new spoke around a corner and back again was never going to help performance.

Somehow, my slightly botched job lasted for nearly 5,000 miles, at which point I was in the US and it was more than just a spoke that gave way (here's an excerpt from my blog):

Day 127 – Newport to Newberg

...the main issue with today came after about 75 kilometres, when I discovered my rear wheel had buckled. I don't remember hitting anything, so it may actually have been that way for a while, but, either way, it was not very amusing. I set about trying to fix it, but after 20 minutes I had made no progress. There weren't any spokes that were noticeably looser, so it wasn't the easiest thing to do... replacing a broken spoke would have been an easier task.

Anyway, I headed on to a bike shop, and was very pleased when they said they would have it sorted in half an hour. Predictably, my joy was short-lived, as, after a few kilometres of riding, it had returned to wobbling all over the place. This means my ego isn't so badly wounded as even a 'proficient' mechanic couldn't fix it, but it does mean I still have a dodgy wheel.

I made another attempt this evening, but I think I'm making it worse. I have 25 miles to Portland tomorrow, where I'll get it properly looked at.

Hopefully, tomorrow's update will be a bit more positive...

Please note, some of my blog excerpts included in this book have been slightly tweaked so that they no longer read as though a four-year-old wrote them.

The next day, I set off for Portland feeling a bit pessimistic about my situation. I was due to meet the guys from Showers Pass (specifically, the owner, Kyle Ranson) for breakfast once I arrived in the city. Showers Pass provided the majority of my wet-weather gear, and I would thoroughly recommend them. I'll mention them a few times, as their kit is fantastic and customer service unparalleled. (That is not a paid endorsement.)

I had breakfast with Kyle, and then he diagnosed my problem. It transpired that the wheel itself had cracked (something I should have noticed myself), so, no matter how much I fiddled with the spokes, it was not going to improve.

Kyle took me to a bike shop that was able to build me a new wheel in 30 minutes (I was still eager to hit 90 miles that day). Kyle and that mechanic 'saved my ass', to coin an American term. Not only that, but he also paid for the new wheel, despite my protests. I owe a lot of thanks to Kyle, and many others at Showers Pass for that matter. Particularly, Kyle's brother, Fraser. He remains a firm friend after offering constant support throughout my trip.

I would have been stuffed without the new wheel, and the rushed build was necessary for my plans; however, a wheel built in that time period was always going to present a few difficulties, especially carrying the weight of my panniers. Over the next 34 days, I got six broken spokes. Hence, I had to have another new wheel sent out to me in Lisbon – this one from the guys at Condor. Many thanks to Jaz at Condor for that.

Thankfully, my final two weeks passed by without any mechanical issues, excluding when the 'support' car broke down after I met Dad, Henry and Nige.

BEHIND THE SCENES:
PART 1

The idea of this challenge first came to me in a school assembly, whilst not listening to whoever was on stage speaking. I think it's safe to say that almost everyone in that hall also had their minds on other things. I was 17 at the time and halfway through my penultimate year at school. By this point, I had already decided that I wanted to take my bike to different destinations around the world in my year before university. I had also realised that flying to lots of exotic places could prove logistically challenging and expensive. I had pinpointed a handful of destinations on a map, but I wasn't sure how I would travel between them.

Whilst dreaming up a way to get around this problem, I came up with the idea of joining up the dots with a bike and cycling between places. My idea developed from there, and the trip that ensued turned out to be 10 times more logistically problematic than my original idea.

I was slightly embarrassed the first time I told my parents about my plans. I was speaking to Mum when she mentioned that I should start thinking about what I wanted to do in my gap year. I had come up with the idea to cycle around the world a few weeks prior to this, and had already started to plan a rough outline for it. I told her my plan, and I suspect she was a little taken aback. Regardless, she remained calm (as always) and said that I should start looking into the logistics of it – probably hoping that I would go off the idea in a week or so. I told her I had already done so, and that I thought it was possible.

No one brought the subject up for close to a week, until my dad asked me if I was serious about the whole thing. Rather sheepishly, I admitted I was. I always felt a bit silly when people asked me about it, even when I was on the brink of departure. I was worried that people would pay no attention and simply see me as a naive and overly ambitious kid. That's exactly what I was, but it took me a long time to realise that this was no bad thing. If everyone thinks your targets are manageable, then they're not challenging enough. That is not gospel; it is just something that I have found to be true with several of my endeavours.

I don't know what my parents said to each other when I wasn't there. I am sure they wished I would just stick to Europe, but, to my face, they were behind me 100%. They never doubted me, not once encouraged me to aim smaller, and always believed in me. When I told my dad I was serious about my idea, he just smiled and said that we should start planning straight away. He was serious too. He wasn't merely playing along with my fantasy; both my parents were instantly committed to my cause.

Enter Mum:

"I first realised he was completely serious when he announced it to his grandparents at a family birthday celebration. When I told some of my friends of his plans, they were horrified and said I shouldn't let him do it!"

Their belief in the plan hit home on my 18th birthday. Six months on from my initial announcement, we had made some progress on the planning and had a reasonable idea of what had to be done, but nothing was concrete. I had no real commitment to the trip, and I could still have backed out easily if I had wanted to. That changed when my parents said they would buy my bike for the trip as my 18th birthday present. Excluding the obvious financial benefit of this, the gesture meant a massive amount to me. They had supported me right from the start, but it was then that I realised they were totally behind me. It was a commitment that demonstrated their belief in me, and that was the best present I could ever have received. Not only that, but it made my idea a reality. Up to that point, it had felt like nothing more than a concept; I never fully believed it would actually happen. The commitment from my parents dispelled those fears, and, from then on, there was no backing out. Despite spending the day at school, I had an ear-to-ear grin the whole time.

A common misconception is that I did all this on my own. Whilst, technically, I did do it solo and I was alone on the road, I still had constant support from back home. I'm not referring to the friends and family who provided huge amounts of moral support through the means of social media. Here, I am referring to the logistical and often emotional side of things.

There were lots of people who offered assistance in one way or another, but the two who organised almost everything, and essentially made my trip into their full-time jobs, were my parents. They were constantly on call to aid me with whatever was needed. Even before I left they were helping me, and the whole thing would never have got off the ground without them. On my own, I would not have had a clue where to begin.

Before I set off, I spent the autumn school term (September to December) working as a teaching assistant at Hornsby House

School in Balham. Those four months were when the majority of the planning was carried out and the logistics sorted. The year before that, whilst I was still in school, had been spent getting a rough idea of what needed to be done.

I owe a special thank you to everyone at Hornsby House – the staff, pupils and parents. I thoroughly enjoyed my time there, learnt a lot, and the support I received from them once I'd set off was amazing. I believe they even had a map in one of the classrooms pin-pointing where I was and following my progress. Not only that but Alex Salandin and Sophie Boucher helped Mum to coordinate everything from media to balloons on my final return in London, which was hugely appreciated.

Along with the planning, training was my other priority. I didn't go crazy; since I was working full time, there was no way that I could put in 100-mile days back to back. Instead, I had to increase the intensity of my efforts, and just accept that the first month or so would be spent getting accustomed to the mileage. I also did not cut out alcohol – something I had done before and have done since for fairly long periods when training for something specific. I could feel the pressure building (which was very much self-inflicted), and I didn't feel the need to add to that by introducing another restriction. That is not to say I drank excessive amounts mind you.

To be perfectly honest, I didn't cycle as much as you would expect – perhaps two or three times a week. A lot of my training was done off the bike. I was aware that I would be spending a lot of time on my bike in the near future, and I did not want to risk falling out of love with it beforehand. This meant I spent time training on and around some pull-up bars with my mate Gus, who was also working at Hornsby House. Often, we did early morning sessions before work – generally a mix of bodyweight and cardio sessions, with the occasional trip to the gym for some squats.

Once a week, the school held a running club before classes for the students. Gus and I would help lead that, after having done up to an hour of our own training already. For me, it was as much about building mental toughness as it was physical. I knew that this was going to play a bigger role than my fitness on the more challenging days. As the winter progressed, I grew to love those freezing mornings – something that definitely served me well.

THE CHARITIES

Raising money for charity was not in my mind when I originally came up with the idea for the challenge. It was only when I started to think a little more about my plans that I realised it was an opportunity I could not waste. More than that, it gave my trip a purpose beyond my own personal gain, and provided a huge motivational boost in some of the harder moments. I received an email every time somebody made a donation, and it meant a massive amount to me to have so many people invest so much in my endeavours, especially early on when even I was doubting my abilities.

After much thought, I eventually decided I would do the ride in aid of three charities – Prostate Cancer UK, Cure EB (formerly called Sohana Research Fund) and Carney's Community.

To me, Prostate Cancer UK needs no explanation. It is an illness that affects millions, and, compared to some other cancer charities, it is very much underfunded.

Cure EB is less well known. The daughter of one of Dad's colleagues – Sohana Collins – suffers from a rare skin condition called recessive dystrophic epidermolysis bullosa, and her parents set up the charity to help find effective treatments and a cure for all those suffering from the disease. Because this rare genetic condition affects relatively few people, the government does not fund research into it. The work done by Sharmila and James Collins is amazing, and there is a real potential for finding a cure for the disease. I actually rode very close to where one of the lead researchers lives in Minnesota, but unfortunately didn't really have to chance to stop by. Sohana herself is incredible. She was 12 when I was first introduced to her, and already one of the strongest and most inspirational people I have ever met. The pain that she and other EB sufferers go through on a daily basis is unimaginable.

The third was Carney's Community: a smaller charity based in my local area in South London. It focuses on turning around the lives of underprivileged young people. Children who are born into a life that presents very few opportunities are driven towards crime and antisocial behaviour through having no other option. Carney's Community aims to get disadvantaged and excluded young people off the street and away from a life of crime, by giving them skills, discipline and self-respect. They use boxing as a way of channelling their minds into something they enjoy, and which is both mentally and physically stimulating and beneficial. For me, supporting Carney's Community was a way to help those around me who are missing out on the opportunities that I have been given. Whilst cycling round the world was far from easy, I would be foolish to overlook the fact that I am extremely fortunate to be in a position to even attempt it.

THE START LINE:
DAYS 1 & 2

Eventually, the time came when the preparations had to stop, and I actually had to ride my bike. Days 1 and 2 could not have been more different.

Day 1 was easy; Day 2 was not.

I was not overly nervous on the first morning, despite the fact that our kitchen was filled with family and close friends, who had come to see me off. Emotions were running high, I think, but I felt oddly withdrawn from the whole situation, as if all the attention was misplaced. I also had a number of cycling mates along to ride out of London with me. I kept telling myself it was a normal weekend ride, and nothing to get worked up about. The second morning was a different matter. I woke up on a ferry after only a few hours' sleep, alone and absolutely terrified.

Both days were cold. Setting off from London it was about 2°C, but, thankfully, sunny. The following day in France offered temperatures the wrong side of freezing, and it rained for the entire day. Except for when it snowed.

Dad and Nige rode the whole way with me on Day 1, after the other cyclists had peeled off outside London. We stopped for dinner with some friends in Portsmouth that evening, with Mum and Anna driving down to join us. There were 11 people round the dinner table, and it was perfect for keeping my mind off the task ahead; not to mention the fact I got a hot shower and a really good meal (many thanks to Jane and Johnny for the wonderful hospitality). In contrast, my dinner the next night was a plate of cold meats and pâté. I was in the middle of nowhere, and that's all the hotel could offer me.

Inevitably, the high spirits from dinner changed when we left for me to catch my 10pm ferry across the Channel. There was nowhere to hide now, and it was time to say goodbye. I would see Dad in a week's time, but I wouldn't see Mum and Anna until April. We didn't prolong the farewell. There wasn't much that needed to be said. I think Dad may have asked me if I was sure about what I was doing. I may have just laughed in reply; I don't remember. If I had said yes, I would have been lying. All I had to do was ride my bike. How hard could it be?

Very, as it turned out. I got about five hours' sleep on the ferry, and then set off on the other side, in the dark and in the rain. The first two hours of Day 2 successfully wiped out the highs of the previous day and any motivation from the novelty of it all. I became progressively more miserable throughout the course of the day, and it ended up being one of the hardest I had ever had on a bike.

Around the three-hour mark, I stopped and looked around. I am still not sure what I wanted or expected to see. I was struggling; the temperature was below freezing, and I was completely soaked. I stood there for a couple of minutes trying to decide what to do, until I realised that I actually only had two options: 1) 'man up' and carry on cycling, or 2) stay where

I was and freeze to death. There was no other choice. I couldn't just call it a day and head home, nor could I ring my parents in search of a lift (not that I have ever done that). So, I carried on riding, having achieved nothing but making myself colder.

Lunch that day was also a bit of an ordeal, and a stark contrast to 24 hours earlier when we'd stopped for a relaxed mid-ride pizza. The people of rural France adopt a similar approach on Sundays to Italians on their lunch break. Other than the boulangeries, nothing was open. I therefore spent the day eating pastries, exclusively.

I ate my lunch underneath an old bandstand. Had this happened later in the trip, I would have got over my inhibitions and eaten my food propped against the counter I had just bought it from. However, only a few hours into my excursion, I still maintained a slight sense of dignity and ate my food elsewhere, on the basis that I was not a savage.

There are very few occasions when I have been as cold as I was then. The combination of the wind, the wet and the Arctic temperatures meant I was shivering so much that I was struggling to get the food in my mouth.

Despite the lack of a proper meal ahead of me, the sense of relief when I reached my finishing point for the day was immense. I proceeded to spend much of the evening attempting to dry my shoes with a hair dryer.

WIND

Regarding my blog, I have mentioned it briefly, and I hope the concept is fairly self-explanatory. Whilst I was riding, I made a point of writing a few bits down and posting them online. This is a fairly common thing to do, but where the majority of people tend to post updates on a weekly to monthly basis, I did it daily. Despite this being a massive pain in the arse, I'm very glad I did it this way. I think one of the key reasons for this, when looking back, is authenticity. All of the updates were written in the heat of the moment, whilst emotions were still running high, and I think that this gives a far more accurate depiction of what I was feeling at each point.

As I have already mentioned, the blog is still available to read. However, if you are considering doing so, please be aware that it was written by a very disgruntled teenager and it is far from a literary masterpiece. Mind you, I hope you're not expecting a masterpiece from this book either.

If you have glanced over my online entries or followed them at the time, you will have realised that one of the downsides of posting every day is that there's a substantial amount of repetition. Of a few recurring themes, there is one that popped up in the vast majority of the updates: wind direction (specifically, headwinds). I cannot deny that I went on about the wind far too much, not least because I was told this by more than a few of the regular readers over the course of my trip. I do, however, want to avoid boring people with it this time round as well. On that basis, I am going to try my best to avoid mentioning the wind on every page. That being said, it seems only fair that I dedicate a short chapter to the subject, as headwinds played such a large part in my cycle. To back up this point, upon my return to England, one friend showed up wearing a white beanie with *"HEADWIND"* written crudely across the front in felt tip. It was funny at the time, but perhaps you had to be there.

I experienced headwinds (and the misery that comes with them) right from the off. As soon as I started in France, I had an icy breeze blowing me back the way I had come. As every cyclist knows, this is annoying at the best of times.

The wind dictated my mood. If I had a tailwind, it was a good day. If I had a tailwind and it wasn't raining, it was a really good day. However, as soon as the wind switched round, my mood would turn sour. There were a handful of days when I managed to rise above it, but not many.

When I first planned my route, riding east seemed to be the preferable choice. It is the more popular way to go round the world, due to the prevailing winds, but it was also favourable for me considering all the different climates I would encounter. In theory, if someone rides east, they will have a tailwind more often than a headwind. I experienced the exact opposite. Of the windy days I had, over two-thirds of them were against me. And, yes, I was sad enough to go through my entire blog and make an Excel spreadsheet to verify this detail.

The overwhelming feeling I had when facing a headwind was frustration. The knowledge that I would ordinarily be going

significantly faster for the same amount of effort was difficult to shake. Riding with panniers was also an absolute nightmare, unless the wind was directly behind me, as they acted as a sail and made matters twice as bad.

As I said at the start, I don't want to dwell on this. I moaned about it enough at the time, and I will no doubt bring up the subject again when I talk about Europe and the long, straight roads in Australia. For now, hopefully, I've got my point across – I had a shit time with the wind.

KNEE TROUBLES

Keeping with the subject of lingering grievances, I had a recurring knee problem, which, aside from the wind, had the largest negative impact on my trip. Training for an around-the-world cycle posed a few problems. Although I put in a lot of hours training in preparation, it was impossible to replicate the task I was about to embark on. Even if I hadn't been working full time, it would have been a challenge to fit in over seven hours' cycling every day around the planning that had to be done. In fact, it's difficult to fit that many hours into unemployed life, regardless of any extra commitments. So, whilst I knew that from a fitness perspective I was able to cycle 100 miles with legs that were already tired from previous days, I had no way of knowing how my body would respond to the task in practice. It was therefore not much of a surprise when I did encounter some injuries. Having said that, I did not anticipate such an injury to keep showing up for the entire time I was away.

Over the first five days of the trip, my knee felt as though it aged about 80 years, and by the morning of Day 6 I was a whimpering mess. I first felt it on Day 3. It wasn't painful, and I barely gave it any thought, but it was there. I could already feel that something wasn't quite right. On Day 4 it became a slight niggle. On Day 5 it started to hurt. The first hour was uncomfortable. It was nothing that I couldn't put up with, but it was not so insignificant that I could just ignore it. The pain then vanished until the final hour or so when the road headed uphill. Amongst the other problems I faced that evening, including snow, my knee limited me to about 70% capacity.

Day 6 was one of the three hardest days of the entire trip. I could tell something was wrong as soon as I woke up. The knee that had been moderately painful the evening before had tightened up during the night and was now excruciating. I went to grab breakfast as usual, but I couldn't bend my leg and could barely walk.

I spent ages trying to decide what to do that morning. After calling my aunt (who is a physio), and conducting my own diagnosis via Google, I made the decision to stay where I was and rest. It was the only logical thing to do. However, at some point during the following 30 minutes, I changed my mind. I don't really know why, but before I knew it, I was heading to the door. Predictably, it was snowing, and the receptionist took great amusement in the fact that I was going to try to ride my bike through it. I can't say I appreciated his jovial tone all that much.

The ride started with a climb, and a steep one at that. It would have been unforgiving, considering the weather, even if my body hadn't been falling to pieces. As it was, it remains the most painful thing I've ever experienced. It felt like someone had stuck a knife under my knee cap. That may sound like a bit of an exaggeration, but I can't think of a better way to describe it. The fact that it was entirely self-inflicted somehow made it worse, given that I could stop any time I wanted. I set myself a one-hour target, and did anything from pedalling one-legged, to shouting my head off to get there. Every minute I told myself to turn around and go back to the hotel, and every minute I knew there was some part of my brain that would never let me do that. I had set out to push myself, and – although I never really expected to go through anything like that, let alone in the first week – I was never going to give up.

Mercifully, after my second stop two hours in, I found that I could actually pedal. The pain had eased up a small amount. This trend continued for much of the next few months. My knee would go through good and bad periods. When going through a bad period, the first hour would always be the worst. It never again reached the extremes that it did on Day 6, but, after a quick stop, I would always find my leg to have loosened up. In this first instance, it was still painful, but, rather than needing to shout expletives, I could get by just by gritting my teeth.

Injuries like this are commonplace in ultra-endurance events, and the sensible thing to do is to stop and rest the afflicted body part. As I have mentioned, it is difficult to know exactly how your muscles and joints will fare when it comes to the real thing. Tight muscles ultimately proved to be the root cause of my problem, although having my cleat set up in the wrong position for a short while was also a contributing factor. Weirdly, I would sometimes spend up to 45 minutes working on my legs with a spikey ball (the same principle as using a foam roller) in the evenings, and I'd wake up in more pain than when I went to bed. This meant I never had any real faith in stretching or massaging whilst I was away, and most of the time I opted not to bother with it. Instead, I told myself to man up and embrace the pain.

I think the climate played a large part in making Europe the worst period for my knee. Warmer weather seemed to help my muscles and tendons loosen, so the pain wasn't quite so noticeable or frequent later on.

It became a significant hindrance again in the final few days of Australia, whilst heading over the Great Dividing Range. I then had it diagnosed by a physio in Brisbane as acute ITB friction syndrome. I didn't know what that meant, but she told me it wouldn't be permanent as long as I was vigilant about stretching, and that set my mind at ease. I already knew my IT band was extremely tight, so I just had to keep working on that, my hamstrings and my hip flexors. I owe a huge thank you to Michael and Jo Dalgleish for seeing me that evening. I showed up at their house at very short notice and with numerous ailments that needed attention.

Even now, my knee flares up from time to time, but a decent amount of stretching normally does the trick; my hip flexors being the crucial muscles. I saw a physio for a few sessions before I left (about some non-knee-related niggles), and he said it was unlikely that I would be able to cycle around the world in the state I was in – referring to my lack of flexibility. He said it jokingly, but, in fairness, he wasn't far wrong. I stretched every day for a long time after those sessions (before leaving) and still encountered numerous problems.

The worst pain I experienced was thankfully short-lived, but came towards the end of North America, on Days 156 and 157. I have no idea what it was or why it came on so suddenly, but for a few minutes on each of those days, I couldn't straighten my leg. It was alright when I was cycling – the bottom of the pedal stroke was essentially the extent of my movement (which I suppose is lucky) – but any time I went to try to lock it out it was agony.

Anyway, that's another topic I moaned about a lot in my blog. In theory, I won't need to mention it again after this.

CHRIS LUBWAMA

Along with my blog, I also updated a Facebook and Twitter page as I went. Over these three social media platforms, I received all manner of comments from other people. I would often receive questions (varying in degrees of intelligence), but the majority of the comments tended to follow the lines of either encouragement and flattery, or comedic insults.

These comments would frequently pick me up when I was having one of my many miserable moments, and I have a lot of people to thank for this. Notably, Fraser Ranson (head of Showers Pass UK), Peter Carden (my sister's godfather), and Will Smith (not the actor and often writing under the alias of his lovely wife, Charlotte). All were regulars to the reply section of my Facebook page or blog, and all provided constant and invaluable encouragement throughout the trip. Then, there was Chris.

Chris Lubwama is another of my dad's old school mates (he was the one wearing the *"HEADWIND"* hat), and, three days into my trip, Chris decided that he would commit to posting a 'thought for the day', every day that I was away.

In Chris' words:

"According to Sara [his other/better half], there is no way I can say something sensible once a day. But she reckons if I restrict myself to stupid comments, apparently I could post every five minutes!"

So, that is exactly what he set out to do. It turned out to be quite a challenge, and considering the length of my trip, it's not surprising that some of the places his thoughts drifted off to were a bit risqué. I found them very amusing, so I feel that it is only right to share some of them with you throughout this book. A large majority of his posts probably push the boundaries of political correctness too far for me to include, but, hopefully, the others will provide sufficient comic relief.

My plan is to include any comments that I found amusing, so they won't all be from Chris; he does deserve a special mention though. His opening remark was this: *"Remember – testicles are not just for Xmas, they're for life. Look after them!"*

He later posted the following disclaimer, which I shall now use to cover my own back:

"Disclaimer – This jocular nonsense was prepared by Chris Lubwama Esq. in his personal capacity as 'idiot savant'. The warped views expressed are solely those of the original author, except those nicked from far cleverer people. These views and opinions do not in any way represent those of any member of the esteemed and venerable Davies family. (Please also note that no animals were harmed in the transmission of this message other than the monkey sitting at the typewriter with electrodes attached to his nether regions.)
"Chris, 28th Feb"

CLOTHING & KIT LIST

On my website, there was a page dedicated to my kit list, which never got finished. When I first made the website, departure was still a way off, so I simply wrote:

Kit list coming soon...

During the final weeks of 2014 I added:

Due to the fact that I'm extremely organised, the final contents of my panniers are yet to be decided. Please stick around for an update nearer my departure...

(That was sarcastic in case you didn't catch on.) I later followed it up with this:

It's now three days until my departure, so I figured I should make some progress with this; the current list is as follows:
      - Two pairs of boxers (I've toyed with the idea of only taking one pair, but it would be a tragedy if I were to lose them).
      That is all.

I never wrote anything more than that. Aside from an inherent laziness, there were a couple of reasonable excuses for this. First and foremost, I didn't actually decide on the final contents of my panniers until I packed them for the last time on the eve of my departure.

The other reason is that my kit list was constantly changing. I carried a variety of different clothes depending on the climate I was in, so it was difficult to write a definitive list, especially ahead of time.

Over three years later, I'm not sure I could tell you everything that I took with me, and – whilst some may want to know – trust me, there really wasn't anything overly exciting or groundbreaking. I should, however, be able to tell you what I wore as I went round.

On my first time through Europe, I had a lot of layers to carry, and I was often wearing most of them. Full winter attire consisted of cycling shorts, cycling-specific leggings, waterproof trousers from Showers Pass, a synthetic base layer, a Merino-wool base layer, a cycling jersey, a Showers Pass jacket, a neck-buff thingy and a hat under my helmet. On my feet I had waterproof socks, some winter cycling shoes (which I'm not convinced made much difference aside from adding weight) and waterproof overshoes. On my hands, I either had a thin set of gloves paired with a waterproof outer set, or I wore a very thick pair akin to skiing gloves. Whichever option I went for, they never seemed to be warm enough; especially when things got wet. So, despite burying myself in clothes, I still spent many of those snowy hours wondering whether it might be worth wetting myself just to warm my legs up.

India, with its shorts-and-T-shirt weather, was a drastic change. I still wore cycling shorts, but I wore a pair of gym shorts over the top and started the stint in a normal cotton T-shirt. I wasn't sure how acceptable wearing just Lycra would be, so I played it safe. I later swapped the T-shirt for a cycling jersey, and I stayed like this through Burma until I took the gym shorts off in Thailand. If you're facing a similar quandary, you will be fine in Lycra I'm sure. I turned heads regardless; I just felt a bit more comfortable.

Australia was a mix between Europe and Asia. I had to cater for wet weather, but I didn't bother with the waterproof trousers or very thick gloves. New Zealand was back to winter, but not quite the extremes of Europe; plus, I had my dad with me, so I didn't have to worry about carrying so much stuff myself.

In North America, I carried the same kit as in Australia, even though much of the continent turned out to be sweltering. California was a surprising exception to this. I expected perfect sunshine from the Golden State, but, instead, I met clouds and chilly temperatures. I actually spent a couple of those first few days getting really cold, because I refused to wear anything but shorts whilst in California. I had been looking forward to stereotypical Californian weather for months, and, unless it started to snow, I wasn't going to dress any differently.

The final leg through Europe was another warm-weather one, and I required little more than my two pairs of shorts and two jerseys.

Aside from clothes, I didn't take very much with me. The most significant item was a laptop. Was it necessary? No. Was I glad I took it? Yes. I used it to write my blog, upload my rides, upload the routes to my Garmin, and if I ever had an hour or two free in the evenings, I could watch a film or something to take my mind off things.

I had some camping gear – a tent, sleeping bag and sleeping mat – but I didn't use any of them all that much, as I will explain later. In a similar vein, and in order to save weight and space, I didn't bother with a camping stove.

Lastly, I had a spikey massage ball, a few portable chargers and some clothes for the evenings – nothing heavy or bulky. That's why I took only two pairs of boxers with me; although that became only one pair for a short while when I lost a pair in Burma – they must have been unwillingly acquired by a hostel owner.

That's about it. I travelled fairly light compared to some people, but, had I been racing, I would have still considered 80% of those things a luxury and left them behind. I wish I'd left behind the pain receptors in my arse.

EUROPE (WINTER):
PART 1

The first few weeks through Europe were the hardest of the whole trip. I've touched on the first two days, the issues with the wind and the issues I faced on Day 6 with my knee. The first week had been getting progressively worse up to that point, where it reached a peak. On Day 7, I had a tailwind and was joined by my dad halfway through. He accompanied me for Day 8 and most of Day 9, and any troubles I had were wiped out on the Côte d'Azur.

The first week felt like the longest of my life, by quite some margin. When I saw Dad halfway through Day 7, I felt as though I'd already been away for a month. That moment had been a target for me since I left the ferry, and, had I not had that meeting to aim for, I would not have got on my bike the morning my knee flared up.

The following 48 hours helped me regain some form of composure. The weather turned good, and the difference having some company made was immeasurable. It was over all too quickly, but, despite Dad having to head back to the airport late in the afternoon, Day 9 remains one of the best of the whole trip.

Day 9

Today was incredible. It was still quite cold, but pretty spectacular. The first 20 miles held one of the best climbs and descents I've ever done. After everything that's happened this past week, I couldn't help but have a massive grin on my face.

From there, the day only got better. Riding through Cannes and then Nice was a bit surreal, and the number of other cyclists was incredible. The view of the Med was an amazing backdrop and it even got warm enough to take my jacket off.

One fairly odd moment came on the Promenade des Anglais when I overtook a cyclist who was pedalling along making motorbike noises. Just goes to show, there are weirdos everywhere – even on the Côte d'Azur!

Dad's takeaway:

"Best sight for me was the 80-year-old woman jogging along the front in Cannes wearing a fur gilet and fur hat! Must have taken a wrong turn out of Hampstead..."

After Dad and I had lunch in Beaulieu-sur-Mer, I headed on towards Monaco – which proved to be a bit of a nightmare to navigate. Nevertheless, I was soon given a very sunny (and uphill) welcome into Italy.

The last stop of the day came in San Remo – quite an iconic place for cyclists. Unfortunately, this is where my dad had to head off back to the airport. Very sad to see him go; it also meant I had to carry all my kit

again! On a serious note, massive thanks to him, these
last two and a half days have been a breeze, and I'm
so glad I was able to spend them with him.

That post does a decent job of summarising the day, but it leaves
out the fact that I spent the 10 minutes after leaving Dad with
tears running down my face, and the last five miles of the day
riding in the dark without a light because I couldn't be bothered
to stop and turn it on.

Generally, I have no problem with leaving family, but the
stress I was under had pushed my emotions through the roof.
As for the lack of a light that evening, unsurprisingly, it made
for a very sketchy finish to the day. Thankfully, Italian drivers
are used to cyclists and were good at avoiding me, but it got to
the point where I was looking at the map on my Garmin to see
when a corner was coming as I couldn't see anything in front of
me. I did not make that mistake again!

Interesting anecdote (to me anyway): the cycle path that I
followed away from San Remo was the same one they used in
the opening team time trial in the Giro D'Italia later that year.

After two days of not riding in Diano Marina, I was
immediately on the back foot again having to deal with food
poisoning for Days 10–12 through northern Italy.

It was Day 11 when the effects of food poisoning really
caught up with me, and even Chris' handy advice did little to
cheer me up that morning:

"Glad to hear you are on the move again, although quite
possibly in more ways than one. Anyway, just for a laugh,
if your stomach is still feeling a bit tricky tomorrow, why
not try a double espresso after every evacuation? Could be
interesting…"

I managed a single mini croissant for breakfast before I thought I was going to be sick again (I didn't bother with the espresso). Getting on the bike, I had almost no energy.

'Bonking' is the term used to describe what happens when your muscles run out of glycogen. Runners tend to call it 'hitting the wall', and it basically refers to a total loss of energy. It is not a pleasant experience, and it is something to be avoided like the plague. Having said that, almost everyone who considers themselves a cyclist will know how it feels. The thing about bonking is that it doesn't just affect your legs, it gets your head as well. You become so exhausted that it's almost impossible to concentrate on anything that is not food or bed related.

Whenever it has happened to me, it has come after not eating enough during a long ride, and is generally followed by riding the shortest route home and eating as much as possible before collapsing on the nearest sofa.

Day 11, in Alessandria, was different. The feeling hit me before I even climbed onto the bike; I was totally empty mentally and physically, yet I could do nothing about it. My body would reject anything I tried to eat, so, instead, I just had to suffer. On that stretch, the Italian landscape was boring and offered no distraction from the fact that I could barely keep my eyes open, let alone pedal. There were no mind games I could play, nothing I could do but stare at the road five metres ahead of my front wheel.

Time ticked by agonisingly slowly. Every 30 seconds or so I would check my Garmin, hoping to see 10 minutes expiring, only to be disappointed.

I had lunch after about 60 miles, in Piacenza. Having eaten nothing since the mini croissant at breakfast, it was necessary. The food would have been unappetising at the best of times, but

I forced myself to eat it. I knew I would barely finish the day if I didn't.

The portion size was similar to what you'd expect from a kids' menu, but it took me almost an hour to eat half of it. I kept feeling myself drift off to sleep as I sat there eating one chip at a time. I ate as much as I could stomach, before heading on once more.

It was well after dark when I finished. It had taken me nine hours to get from door to door, despite the route being totally flat. I was staying in a B&B in a town called Canneto Sull'Oglio.

The joy of finishing did nothing to bring me any energy. Everything seemed to take longer that night, including rinsing my kit in the shower, which I did sitting down. I had hardly eaten since lunch, so I headed out to the closest pizza place.

Going to a restaurant alone is not something people tend to do very often; at least not British teenagers. It's something I have been asked about a surprising amount, and I know a few people who would find it difficult.

During the October before I left, I went on a four-day practice trip to Wales. The second day was Halloween, and I spent the night in Abergavenny. I went for a curry, but I couldn't help but feel rather self-conscious. My friends were out somewhere in London, and I was sitting alone in the Brecon Beacons. My phone then ran out of battery before the food arrived, so there was nothing I could do but sit there pondering life. I'm normally very good at not caring what people think about me, but I did feel slightly out of place that evening. It did not help that I was the first one in the restaurant.

Anyway, once on the road for the real trip, eating alone rarely bothered me. It is far more commonplace in continental Europe, but I often quite enjoyed the quizzical looks I received. The meal in Canneto Sull'Oglio was a bit different. Much like the curry house in Abergavenny, I was the first person in the restaurant, but, unlike the curry house in Abergavenny, no one else arrived for the rest of the time I was there. I also didn't speak the language, which added to the awkwardness of any conversation I had with the waiting staff. When they unveiled one of the largest pizzas I had ever seen, I knew I was in trouble. I had been cycling 100 miles a day for almost two weeks, I should have been able to finish two of them; instead, I only just managed two slices. That was the most embarrassing aspect of it all, but I figured it was better to leave the food than risk another bite and end up being sick all over the table (and in the process lose the few calories I had managed to keep down). I left my dinner feeling guilty. I hadn't even ordered an exciting pizza. Thinking of my stomach, I had ordered a Margherita – not exactly extravagant.

After Day 6, I had quietly hoped that I might have already been through my hardest day. Day 11 was shit, but still a way off that level. Day 14, however, knocked me flat on my arse and reminded me that I still had a very long way to go. It was on a par with the knee problems, if not worse. But, where Day 6 hit me with physical pain, Day 14 pushed my head to the limit.

I can't put my finger on why I found it so arduous. The total riding time was over eight and a half hours, and door to door was just shy of eleven. It was not a case of one thing making it difficult; it was an accumulation of nine hours in rain, wind and snow that led to the final hour being one of the toughest mental battles I faced.

At the time, I didn't know how to write about what happened, and, even now, I still don't. I found myself in a strange place mentally. I think I was merely exhausted, and the elements had completely stripped me of any sanity:

I could see nothing but the light from my head torch, and I felt nothing other than the wind forcing me in

*the wrong direction. If there's a name for whatever
emotion I was feeling, I don't know it.*

*At times, I felt like I was going uphill at walking
pace, and, at others, I came very close to losing
balance. I shouted a lot, at nothing in particular. I
think I may have even started crying at one point;
not of sadness, just determination. Writing this now
it sounds as if I was close to breaking point, but, in
fact, I don't think I've ever been stronger. I apologise
for the philosophical bullshit; my head is in a weird
place this evening.*

That's what I wrote in my blog that evening. It sounds a bit silly
now, but, even with hindsight, I can't expand on it. So there it is.
Day 14, one of the really bad ones.

Day 15 – Senj to Sukošan

*It was hard waking up this morning. I hadn't had as
much sleep as I would've liked, and I'd gone to bed
with it about to start snowing. So, when I finally got
up and looked outside to see a clear Croatian sunrise,
I was more than a bit surprised. By the time I finally
left my room, I was smiling.*

*As soon as I got on my bike, the evening before
felt like a bad dream, and I was loving riding my bike
again. In 15 days, this is only the third or fourth that I
would've regretted missing had I not been on this trip.
It was stunning.*

*The first 20 kilometres held a bit of a climb, but
one that I would gladly do again (although perhaps
on a lighter bike). The road was quiet and of the*

cars that did pass, many gave friendly beeps of encouragement – after riding a lot in London, it's easy to tell this apart from an angry beep. The road was smooth and the view spectacular. Quite frankly, it couldn't have been more different from yesterday.

The views, the road and the weather continued for the next 80 miles, and I couldn't have asked for any more today. My knee is ever improving, my legs felt great and seven hours in the saddle passed relatively easily. The last 15 kilometres were a bit busy as I rode around Zadar, but nothing too bad.

The wind wasn't really in my favour today but it didn't hinder me that much, so I can't complain about it. The few complaints I do have are only minor. My arse hurt more than normal for the first couple of hours, but, to be honest, it's held up well considering what it's been through these last few weeks (that's not as controversial as it sounds). Also, whilst the roads being quiet was a good thing, the towns were also ghostly. I went into one, and it seemed I was the only living thing there. Every single house was boarded up and really quite eerie. This meant I survived the day eating chocolate and bananas that I managed to buy from a handful of mini (very mini) supermarkets.

Anyway, today has been a good day; if you're a cyclist, one to be jealous of. Yesterday is forgotten and I'm looking forward to tomorrow... Although I think it may be raining again.

SELF-DOUBT

I finished Day 10 in Alessandria, Italy, whilst still suffering from food poisoning. The two rest days I'd taken prior to that had hindered me massively, and there had been almost no improvement in the condition of my knee.

In my room that evening, I reached one of my lowest points ever in terms of self-belief. One of my best friends from home had called me, and we spoke for about 20 minutes. Initially, it helped ease my mind – it was always good to hear a familiar voice – but then she asked a question that led to a tsunami of self-doubt. It was obvious I'd had to dig deep. We'd talked about the lousy weather, my buggered knee and my illness, and, completely innocently, she asked me if I regretted doing it.

Out of instinct, I immediately answered no, but, once the call was over, I couldn't get the question out of my head. I think, at that moment, I truly did regret it. I spent the rest of my waking minutes attempting to convince myself that this wasn't the case, doing everything I could to stay positive. By the time I was dropping off to sleep, the best I could manage was, *I don't regret it, but if I were able to go back in time, I would make a different choice for my gap year.* That, to me now, seems pretty close to regret. I remember thinking those exact words, and, at the time, it was just enough to keep me afloat.

That night I had a dream, one that even now (three years later) I remember vividly. I don't normally pay attention to this kind of thing, but bear with me. Disclaimer: my sister would not act like this in real life.

I dreamt that I'd had an accident. That I had been hit by a car, and my bike was written off. The trip was over. I was standing there looking at my broken bike, and my sister was laughing at me; at which point, my dad came over and told her to stop because I was utterly distraught, and it wasn't funny. The weird thing was, I was only pretending to be upset; inside, I was thankful that I had an easy way out of the task ahead.

When I woke up, I felt the same feeling. As I came to my senses and realised that none of those events had actually happened, I was bitterly disappointed. I was sad that my bike wasn't broken, I was sad that my body was in one piece, and I absolutely hated that I had to get out of bed and ride 100 miles.

I only mention this dream because it made me face the fact that I loathed the situation I had put myself in. I was never going to quit, but I really wanted it all to be over.

I think that was my weakest point mentally, and I'm finding it slightly embarrassing to write about it. I had almost given up on myself, and I felt completely vulnerable. Had my bike broken for real, I still don't think I would have stopped – I would never have been able to live with myself if I had – but it was a notion that, for a few hours, I entertained as being a favourable outcome.

These thoughts disappeared at a similar rate to my food poisoning, and two days later I was back to full mental strength. To counter these low points, there were days of unparalleled and misplaced confidence. Through Australia and North America, I repeatedly told myself that if I had a crash and broke a bone,

I would still carry on (unless it was a major part of my leg). In these extreme cases of idiocy, I once again welcomed an accident; however, this time it was to prove that I could carry on despite the pain. In these moments, all I was thinking was how cool it would be if I cycled across a continent with a broken collarbone. I'm not sure how I arrived at a point of being quite so delusional.

ROUTINE

Routine is important in a task like this. It makes things more monotonous, but takes away a lot of the stress. When you have a pattern for waking up, taking breaks, getting food and preparing for tomorrow, far less mental energy is required. At the same time (and this may sound contradictory), it is even more important to be adaptable. When something goes wrong – and, unfortunately, something always will – it is very easy to get frustrated and throw a tantrum, so you have to be able to adjust. For anyone planning something similar, this is one of the biggest pieces of advice I can give. Have a clear plan, but hold on to it loosely. Settle into a rhythm quickly, but don't lose your head when something out of your control changes your plans.

My routine changed throughout the course of the trip depending on the different climates, my fitness levels and the food available. As the months went on, I got better at finding the ideal pattern. That was until I got back to Lisbon; after Australia, New Zealand and North America, I was thrown off guard by the foreign language, and felt like I was back to square one for the penultimate week.

Being adaptable took more time to get used to. I am generally a fairly relaxed person, so I set off from a reasonably good starting point. However, on this trip, I found myself stressing enormously over tiny details. For instance, on the morning of Day 13, I got really pissed off by the fact that my phone was only on 99% charge and not 100%. No clue why.

Over the first two months, I experienced some random and fairly drastic mood swings. Again, this was something I improved on, and, by the time I reached North America, I was able to take some big hits to the chin; for example, the day that my wheel buckled. Yes, I got frustrated, but I dealt with it methodically and handled the situation well. It was convenient that I was only a day's ride from Portland, but, had that happened in Europe at the start, I would have had a hissy fit.

There were moments, of course, when I lost concentration and let the immediate situation get the better of me. Day 139 springs to mind – I heedlessly followed my Garmin the wrong way. I ended up riding 10 miles to a dead end, then had to turn around and go back the same way. I punctured later that day, then a spoke broke as well. On this occasion, I did have a bit of a strop.

Going back to my routine, Europe was the hardest place in which to establish consistency, largely because I was changing country every few days. I tended to stop every hour (which worked out at around 25 kilometres) to have something to eat. Not a full meal, just a chocolate bar or something (Snickers were the favourite until I got sick of them). Under normal circumstances, I would eat whilst riding, but I was always wearing thick gloves in Europe, so I had to stop and take them off.

India was different, and, although the food on offer was of questionable quality, they made up for it in quantity. There were roadside stalls almost every 10 minutes, which meant I was able to plan my stops far more precisely. I opted for a general rule of a stop every 40 kilometres – so three stops a day. I was flexible with this if I needed to be, but that provided a good base to work from and convenient milestones to help break up the day. By the end of India, I was regularly riding further between stops, but I still kept the 40-kilometre mark in mind, because I felt as though I was gaining time whenever I surpassed it.

The abundance of food stalls meant I could pick and choose where I stopped. Having somewhere in the shade to sit was important, but in the busy areas I would sometimes choose (whilst still riding) based on the flavours of crisps they had hanging on the outside.

As for the evenings, it was in India where the habit of buying the following day's breakfast started. I also made a point of buying three litres of water each evening. This tended to cover drinking water overnight, brushing my teeth and then filling my bottles the next day.

In Thailand, I really became a slave to regime. I fell in love with the 7-Eleven shops, which, as is often the case with franchises, all offered the same food. This meant I could eat the same thing every day, and, despite the low quality, I developed a daily craving for toasted ham and cheese croissants. There were other things I bought regularly, but I can't remember what they were; I think one of them involved strawberry jam.

This food was far from healthy, but it provided familiarity in my unpredictable lifestyle, and, realistically, I didn't have to worry about the calories I was consuming. I suppose all I was doing was comfort eating.

When I reached the US a couple of months later, I was reintroduced to 7-Elevens. However, my affinity for them had expired. Instead, I developed a strong love of Subway.

Things changed wherever I went. Even crossing the US border into Canada, I had to switch strategy. Doing so became more challenging at points, like in the Australian Outback, but I would eventually settle into a rhythm regardless of where I was.

I found it weird how annoyed I got when something interrupted my routine. However, once home, it became clear how difficult a habit can be to break. The day after I finished in London, I received a call from the BBC asking if I wanted to come up to Salford to appear on *BBC Breakfast* the next morning. They bought my train ticket and put me up in a hotel near the studio. Without thinking, I went out and bought some food for the morning. It was only when I got back to my room that I realised the hotel provided breakfast – and it had already been paid for. Nevertheless, I ate the food I'd bought anyway, and then went down to the buffet for a second breakfast.

ALCOHOL

It probably won't surprise you to learn that I did not drink very much alcohol whilst away on my trip. It wasn't solely because of the decline in performance that alcohol brings; I generally didn't have the time or the energy to go out and get battered, nor even tipsy.

The majority of my friends were all doing the complete opposite. As far as I was aware, they were either at university and waking up clueless most mornings, or they were in far-off countries partying on beaches and acquiring normal-looking tan lines. I was never overly jealous of the parties per se, but there were times when I was envious of the fact that they were actively enjoying themselves.

People often seem surprised when they ask me if I enjoyed my trip and I answer in the negative. Just to set the record straight, this does not mean that I regret it. I have no regrets about anything I did, and I can confidently say that every single second was worth it. Just because I found the experience largely unenjoyable does not mean that I would swap it for anything else. (It also doesn't mean that I was miserable all of the time; there were some good bits.)

When it comes to alcohol, I think the night I drank the most was in Slano, Croatia. I had spent all day riding through rain, and was staying the night in a small B&B run by an incredibly friendly couple (unfortunately, I have completely forgotten their names). Although it was not normally included in their fee, they took pity on me and gave me dinner as well. This decision was no doubt influenced by the fact that it was out of tourist season and so there were no restaurants open in the small town. Regardless, I appreciated their hospitality hugely.

The wife cooked breaded chicken, spinach and boiled potatoes. It was simple, but exactly what I needed, and tasted really good. Neither she nor her husband spoke much English; he knew just enough to make conversation and she was quite shy. However, it was my first significant amount of human contact I'd had since I said goodbye to my dad in Italy, and I thoroughly enjoyed myself.

I don't remember what dessert was, but I do remember that the husband was very keen to show me his selection of Croatian brandy. I hadn't had any alcohol since New Year's Eve (about a month previously), so this wasn't ideal. I didn't want to appear rude though, so it was difficult to decline. He was already reasonably drunk from the wine he'd been drinking throughout the meal.

Thankfully, nothing turned messy, and, after a few shots, I eventually managed to make my excuses and head up to bed. Admittedly, this is not an overly exciting anecdote, but is something that I think is a good representation of some aspects of the whole trip.

Excluding the odd drink on days off, it wasn't until I reached Australia that I allowed myself a beer in the evenings. I would certainly recommend having the occasional beer if you ever find yourself doing something similar. Once I had reached the southern hemisphere and had settled into my trip a bit, I discovered that beer – in strict moderation – was a great way to relax and replace carbohydrates.

I also stopped shaving (my face) in Australia, so, by the time I was halfway across, I no longer needed to worry about having my ID checked. That was until I got to New Zealand. I had a full beard by this point, was accompanied by my dad and was trying to order a single beer with a meal. Despite this, the waitress/owner in one restaurant still initially refused me service, as I didn't have proof of age with me. I eventually got the beer, but it took far more hassle than it should have done.

The US posed a different problem altogether; I was actually under the legal drinking age there (not being 21), which is ridiculous. I tried my luck on a number of occasions, hoping that my flashy British accent would be enough, but, unfortunately, it never worked. I did manage to convince one person and was given a seat at the bar. However, upon ordering a drink, I was found out and promptly asked to move.

It was brilliant to arrive in Canada and discover the drinking age to be 19.

Anyway, my point from all this is that I did not drink a lot over the course of the six months. I think an assumption that gets taken from that is that a 'normal gap year' didn't appeal to me. That is not the case at all, but it was one or the other. I wouldn't want anyone to view me as one of those perfect teenagers who doesn't drink, does all their homework and wakes up at a respectable hour. I am definitely not one of those. Just a normal guy with a particular fondness for cycling.

As if to demonstrate this, I went to a birthday party within a week of my return, and my 'friends' took great pleasure in highlighting how much of a lightweight I had become. I spent most of the evening face down on the floor. On top of that, I was due to fly to France the next day. To say that the flight was unpleasant would be an understatement, but that experience was a necessary evil. It quickly brought me back down to earth after what had been a surreal portion of my life. After all, you should always be able to count on your friends to keep your ego in check.

EUROPE (WINTER):
PART 2

Following on from the emotional rollercoaster of Days 14 and 15, Day 16 was one of those days totally defined by wind. I will try not to dwell on it, but I did learn an important lesson that day. I was due to stay in Omis (Croatia) for the night, where my parents had booked a massage for me. Whilst this seemed like a good plan when it was made, I quickly discovered a drawback. Having a deadline made things far more stressful. I spent the whole day worrying that I wasn't going to make it, and, with a constant headwind, I got more and more frustrated. It wouldn't have mattered in the slightest had I missed the appointment, but it was easy to get wrapped up in the little things. After that, I avoided telling people I would be somewhere by a certain time as much as possible.

Day 17 was wet, but it was livened up when I met the craziest man on the planet:

...I met him whilst buying some food around Ploče. He looked about as mental as he sounded, and he'd

obviously had his fair share of drink. Despite this, he was completely harmless, and, once he realised I was from Britain, he simply started naming random places around England and Scotland. I think his favourite was Glasgow – he burst out laughing when he mentioned that.

I don't remember much else from the day, although I did have to pop into Bosnia. I saw a couple of very nice views, but I was only there for 34 minutes before crossing back into Croatia, so I didn't see much of the country. It was that evening when I stayed with the nice couple serving brandy.

My transition into Montenegro came on Day 18. I knew nothing of the country apart from what I had seen in *Casino Royale* (the Bond film), which, it turns out, was actually shot in the Czech Republic. The ride itself was a bit shit. The new country kept me interested, but the weather was awful, and the roads were bad:

The difference between the countries [Croatia and Montenegro] was apparent instantly. Montenegro was considerably more 'third world'. (I am aware that's un-PC, but frankly I can't think of a better way to put it). I still haven't completely made my mind up about Montenegro. In short, it was a bit of a culture shock, and not one that I was expecting. It became more developed the further I moved into the country, and someone is clearly pushing to make it the next big holiday destination.

The driving is also interesting. I've been informed that they don't get many cyclists here and it's very apparent. Not many of the cars knew how to deal with me. Some would wait behind unnecessarily, and others would speed by within inches. Luckily, there were only two instances where I had to actively avoid crashing.

Sad to leave Croatia, all the people were extremely friendly, and the country had moments of brilliance. Definitely a place for a summer visit!

I was only in Montenegro for one night, before moving on to Albania, which I am very glad I saw. In a way, it took away from Montenegro slightly. Montenegro is almost exactly what you'd expect from a country between Croatia and Albania. So, what was new and interesting there was instantly trumped by Albania:

Despite the drastic cultural difference between Albania and what I've grown up in, I really liked it straight away, and I much prefer it to Montenegro (so far). I found it fascinating. For the first 10 or 20 kilometres I was cycling through little villages; and, despite the slightly bumpy, road I was thoroughly enjoying it.

There is clearly a lot of poverty in Albania; there's no point dressing it up – there just is. But there seems to be a split when it comes to the style of house in the first few villages I covered. There were the older ones, which were falling apart – and which, quite honestly, wouldn't be fun to live in. Then there were the clearly newer ones. They were still basic, but it's as if everyone is in a competition to make their house as brightly coloured as possible. I've honestly never seen such a wide range of colours being used on houses before. The most popular seem to be either lime green or purple. The one other thing all the houses had in common was a large front gate. The gates are often bigger than the walls around the garden, and, once again, they're brightly coloured and often have intricate designs. This may sound like a strange thing to pick up on, but it's very noticeable.

After this, I hit a slightly bigger town, and from there, I was on what must be one of the main roads in Albania. The road was generally good, and it was still interesting. The cultural differences were noticeable everywhere. All day I've been greeted by strangers – most of them say "Hello"; apparently, it's clear I'm not a local. But all of them wave, and it gets to a point where it's hard to return the gesture. I didn't expect anything like that coming into the country.

I stopped at around halfway, and was approached by a boy who turned out to be only 13, despite being taller than me (although that's not difficult). As he said, and as has become clear, most of the younger generation are almost fluent in English, whereas the adults speak next to none. It's quite odd and very obvious, as no one hesitates to try to talk to you.

I was in a good mood and captivated by Albania. My route then took me on a slight detour off the main road. I turned into a few more villages, and these were a fair bit more poverty stricken. People would still greet me, but the standard of living dropped significantly. The road also deteriorated somewhat, and it was hard to navigate.

Once back on the main road, I quickly came up to the final 25 kilometres. At this point, it started raining again, the light started to go, and the road got busier *as I got closer to Tirana. This trend continued the closer I got to the city.*

Tirana itself is absolutely mental. The traffic is crazy, and I'm glad I've spent time riding round London, otherwise this could have been dodgy. A couple of times I was forced towards large holes in the road or off the road altogether. Once again, there was a massive split between the outskirts of the city and the centre; there's a clear divide in the wealth. The thing that remained consistent was the traffic. It's similar to what I'm expecting from India. It was never clear how many lanes there were meant to be, and people use their horns at every opportunity - although, to be fair, it's often with good reason. Anyway, I made it through, despite an agonisingly slow last five kilometres. The city seems pretty lively, and if it's culture you're interested in, it's probably worth a visit.

I was extremely fond of Albania after my first day there, but, unfortunately, that changed. It wasn't that I started to dislike the country itself, it was more the fact that I started to dislike riding there. Partly because of the roads, or lack of, but mostly because of the dogs. I was chased by them four times over the next 36 hours, and it destroyed my nerves.

When I crossed into Greece on Day 21, I felt a huge sense of relief. That day was deliberately shorter – only 70 miles or so. Dad had planned it to give me a bit of a rest, and I didn't argue. Irritatingly, much like the rest day I took in Italy, it only succeeded in causing further problems.

Initially, it was great. I finished early, got to eat more than usual and was able to relax more than usual. It then snowed all through the night, so my situation wasn't looking great when I woke up. The snow hadn't properly settled on the roads, but it was still falling, and the temperature was around -3°C. I set off in dismal conditions, and, within 20 minutes, my breath had frozen on my neck gaiter, turning it solid.

I reached the top of a half-hour climb after 20 kilometres, and that's where things got bad. The temperature had dropped by another 4°C or 5°C (without including the wind-chill factor), and I suddenly found myself in a blizzard. I had felt the wind whilst riding up the climb, but I hadn't been focusing enough to notice how much harder the snow was coming down.

After a freezing descent down the other side, the wind started blowing across me, and the road iced over. My tyres were sliding out underneath me, and I realised I had to stop riding and try to wait it out. Mercifully, I found a petrol station not far up the road and headed in there. By this point, I was pushing myself along with my feet in order to keep my balance.

I stumbled into the small building, and was met by five or six quizzical looks from the locals. I slumped into the only remaining seat, shivering, and tried to get some feeling into my hands. The woman running the shop came over and poured something over them. I'm not sure what it was, it smelt alcoholic and had a similar effect to deep heat. It made my hands burn, but I don't think it actually did anything to warm the blood in them as I still couldn't use them.

It didn't take me long to realise that none of the people in there spoke any English – and I clearly knew no Greek. I was in a state, the snow was showing no signs of easing, and I had no clue what to do. I kept standing up to go look outside and try to ride, and the locals kept protesting in Greek, telling me to sit back down and relax. I found it really difficult to think rationally at times like this, and I started to fear for the success of the whole trip. I began to worry that this setback could end the entire thing. Worst-case scenario, it would add two days, which, in the scheme of things, was insignificant. I couldn't see that at the time though, and merely became more upset and more frustrated. In reality, it didn't change much at all. I did some longer days at the end of the European leg to make up the lost miles, and still caught the same flight out of Istanbul that I had booked a few days earlier.

After an hour or so, and after a phone call back home, I was convinced by the locals not to ride. The owner/manager (the woman who had the alcohol stuff), gave me a hot meal for free, and without me asking for it, which was extremely generous. I don't think I really appreciated it that much at the time as I was so frustrated. About two hours passed, and after lots of Greek words I realised that I was being offered a lift to a hotel in the next village. I accepted the offer – although I had to wait another hour before the person with a pickup truck arrived. I'm now sitting in a partially heated room, not entirely sure about where my dinner is coming from.

Looking back now, I don't even know if the place I stayed in was actually a hotel, or whether I had been given an unsuspecting woman's bedroom. I paid her, obviously, but I genuinely can't say either way. There was also no way I could have ridden any further. By the time I left the petrol station, still shivering in wet clothes, even the truck had difficulty ploughing through the snow. In that moment, the overwhelming emotion I felt was guilt. I truly felt as though I was letting people down back in England by not hitting my daily target. It's a bit ridiculous, but I got so caught up in it all, and it was one of the few occasions that having a following counted against me. Of course, in reality, no one else minded in the least.

After the roads cleared the next morning, I rode back to the petrol station. Firstly, because I wanted to ride from where I stopped riding the day before; I wouldn't have been satisfied knowing that I skipped part of the route. Secondly, I needed to say thank you properly. I'd been in a real state the previous day, and hadn't fully appreciated what the people there had done for me.

I popped inside to see most of the same faces as the day before – they were visibly very surprised to see me. I said thank you and once again tried to offer money, but again the owner refused. I bought a couple of very mediocre croissants instead, and headed on my way.

The rest of that day was largely frustrating, but when I eventually finished, I was in a good mood. Ice on the roads meant I didn't get away until 1pm, so I didn't manage 100 miles. At the place where I stopped, the guy behind the desk thought I was in my mid-twenties. When I handed over my ID, he looked at it and exclaimed in a thick accent, "Oh! You are little!" That was the first time I got mistaken for being older than I am. Normally, it would be the other way round.

The two following days (24 and 25) were very similar to each other, and, looking back, I struggle to differentiate between the two. Both were longer than normal at 115 miles, both were uneventful, and, in both, my mood was directly represented by the wind direction. So, most of the time I was grumpy. The first of the two did offer something different when I had an interview over the phone for a Greek newspaper. It was organised by a friend of my grandfather, and led to a full-page spread in the local paper. I couldn't understand what it said, of course, but it was nice to be recognised. Day 25 was my last full day in Greece, so here are my thoughts on the country that I wrote at the time:

> As for my Greek experience, it's coming to an end tomorrow, so I thought I'd mention that, so far, the people here have been the most generous I've encountered. I've been given free food on three occasions, and everyone has been genuinely interested in my trip. The weather has put a downer on the whole thing unfortunately. I've been fighting a headwind since Venice, but only here was I actually unable to ride due to the weather. The drivers have always attempted to be good to me, but they are often pretty rubbish. Furthermore, the Greek roundabout system is broken, and, whilst there are a number of money troubles to fix, I personally think the new prime minister should address this issue first. That sums up how much thought I'm giving to politics right now.

The following is friend-of-the-family Will Smith's response to my incessant moaning about the weather:

> "Well done Thomas, good work. Hope you have a great day today. The erudite descriptions of coping with the vicissitudes of your journey make for essential reading, and I look forward to reading the grumpings about spending a weekend in Istanbul with the social headwind that is your father."

It made me laugh.

Chris also had a different view of the country:

"Whilst you are making your big, final push, there are a few loose ends to tie up for me here. The Island of Mykonos is said to have been the location of a great battle between Zeus and Titan, and where Hercules killed these allegedly invincible giants, having lured them from Mount Olympus. Legend has it that the large rocks all over the island are their petrified testicles."

Day 26 was the final day of my European winter leg. I was due to meet Dad somewhere along the road in Turkey; the border of which came 30 miles into the day. I had a horrendously frustrating first three hours into the wind. I was pushing hard and averaging 11 miles per hour. This meant I was running late, but, out of pure coincidence, I got through border control at exactly the same time as my dad pulled up in a car:

I can't really put into words how it felt to see him. I suddenly realised the emotional and mental strain I've put myself under this last few weeks, and I don't think I've ever felt such a drastic switch in emotions

I cried like a little baby. I've never felt such a cathartic release. All the emotions that had built up over the prior weeks came pouring out as soon as I saw him. I couldn't do anything to stop myself; I felt an overwhelming sense of relief, and I don't think I have ever been so emotional.

I still had close to 70 miles to do. The ride was really shit. It was cold and windy. The road was shit, and the views were shit. But I didn't care. By the time I finished, I had already got my tears out, but the relief was still there. I felt little else. I was just glad to be done with what remains the hardest four weeks of my life.

Europe was the most demanding leg of all. Mostly, it was down to the weather and a few unfortunate events; however, I think what I went through there toughened me up. I think that the main reason I found it so difficult, comparatively speaking, is because I was mentally and physically capable of enduring far more after those experiences. If I hadn't had the problems on Day 6 or Day 14, or been ill in Italy, I would have faced similar battles later on. Almost everything the world would throw at me (except for heat), I encountered at some point within those first four weeks. In essence, Europe was a very intense acclimatisation. It was perhaps like climbing Everest as preparation for climbing Ben Nevis 100 times. I have done neither, but, essentially, the majority of the challenge was still ahead, even though everything I was forced to adapt to in Europe prepared me for what was to come.

WILDLIFE
ENCOUNTERS

I had a few run-ins with various animals over the course of my ride. Some were good; some were bad. The sight of a cyclist seemed to trigger a fight or flight reflex in them, regardless of the country or species. I'm not sure why that was, although a strong argument could be made for the fact I smelt pretty bad – something I got used to, but I'm sure others found fairly offensive at times.

DOGS

Dogs were the worst. Even in England, they seem to take exception to bicycle riders, and this continued throughout Europe. In countries such as England and France, I never received more than an angry bark. The further east I headed, the more hostility they showed. I was first chased by them in Montenegro. I knew it would happen; almost everyone who has done a similar ride has experienced it, so I wasn't surprised when I eventually encountered some more aggressive dogs. Despite the prior warning, I didn't really know how to deal with them. Some people resort to carrying a stick on their bike, which they can whip out and brandish like a sword. This is something I would have done, if it wasn't for the impracticality of carrying it. I simply decided to try to cycle faster than they could run.

I crossed into Albania from Montenegro later that day, and the next morning, after heading out of Tirana, I discovered the flaw in my method. The road headed uphill, straight out of the city, and it was on this climb that I realised I wasn't going fast enough, should I bump into any dogs. Thankfully, most of those I saw as I ascended through the villages were chained or caged up. I'm not sure how they knew I was coming, but they would always start making a fuss before they could see me (perhaps it genuinely was the smell). Unfortunately, I did eventually come across a pack of dogs that were not chained up. It was a group of four, and they were not friendly. It scared me shitless. Obviously, it was far from pleasant, but it wasn't an overly dangerous situation, and I was surprised by how little composure I maintained.

Another common method for dealing with barking animals is to kick them. However, in my state of panic, I decided that, although this may deter the one I would hopefully connect with, it would do little to change the minds of the other three. Not only that, but I would slow down if I took a foot off the pedal. So, I therefore stuck to my idea of pedalling fast, and hoped that they wouldn't bite whilst my legs were moving.

This happened a few more times that day, all on long, uphill sections. The final encounter was the worst. I was on an open and exposed climb, and saw the dogs about 100 metres up the mountain. I started riding faster as soon as they began to run towards me, but felt a glimmer of hope as I noticed there was a four-metre drop from the bank they were on down to the tarmac.

Unfortunately, they were so determined to get to me, that all six of them jumped down onto the road without hesitation. Shouting at them was useless, and my theory of spinning my legs worked to an extent, but it didn't stop one of them jumping up in an attempt to take a chunk from my arm. Nor did it stop them almost running into my wheels, which would have made me crash. I have since been told that if you stop and get off your bike, they will realise you're just a human and won't be so aggressive. I'm not entirely convinced by this theory, and if it ever happens again, I won't be experimenting with it, especially not somewhere with a risk of rabies.

The dogs eventually left me alone, but my nerves were ruined, and I was constantly on edge until I crossed into Greece the next day. I still experienced minor dog problems there and in Turkey, but never as bad as in Albania. It's a shame because it spoilt my otherwise positive feelings towards the country.

Dogs, luckily, weren't an issue in India. They were everywhere, but they must have all been exhausted from the heat and lack of food. If I did upset them, they couldn't be bothered to act on it. Thailand was the final time any dogs made a genuine effort to bite me, and it was here that I finally came up with the idea of squirting them with water. I was always carrying a bottle on my bike anyway, so it was the perfect defence. Once, it worked so well that I made a dog trip over its front legs and do a front flip – something I found very amusing at the time.

Enter Chris:

"Dog squirting sounds like fun. It may even have potential as a fully fledged Olympic sport! I recently took part in something similar, which turned out to be even more fun. Sara's mum has a cat, called Pickle, which has a proclivity for feet and shoes, upon which it likes to pounce, bite,

gnaw and chew, occasionally taking a chunk out of your ankle. I found that the best way to gently dissuade him from this irritating activity was to employ the use of my mid-body waste fluid removal device – and urinate on his head. Worked every time, but I appreciate it might be a bit difficult for you to follow suit without getting off your bike..."

The only other canine-related anecdote I have is that I saw a dog get run over in India (Day 40). I had stopped to refuel and was sitting on the pavement when a dog wandered obliviously into the path of an equally oblivious driver. The latter didn't bat an eyelid and carried on his merry way. The dog started howling its head off. You know that hideous sound foxes make in the night? Well, it was like that, only five times more annoying, plus I felt genuinely sorry for it. There wasn't anything I could do though. The locals seemed unconcerned, as if it happened all the time. Perhaps the dog was exaggerating a bit because, after 10 minutes, it suddenly stopped limping and shut up. It reminded me of when footballers pretend to be hurt.

COWS

Cows, for the most part, presented absolutely no trouble at all. The vast majority of those I saw were in enclosed fields, and did nothing other than occasionally raise a head as I rode by.

These peaceful beasts, that I was usually happy to see, behaved rather differently in India. There, I realised they are some of the most idiotic creatures walking the earth. Cows are sacred in India, which means they are generally free to roam around and do whatever they please. This is often nothing – it just becomes quite frustrating when they decide to do *nothing* in the middle of the road. I had been led to believe that you aren't even allowed to touch cows in India, but the locals would often hit them if they decided to hold up the traffic for too long.

I would regularly find myself getting annoyed with an overly sedentary cow, and I would often come close to getting knocked off by them. They wander into the road as if nothing is going on around them, and with no regard to any danger that could come their way. Having said that, this seems to apply to the Indian drivers as well, so perhaps they're just following the drivers' example.

The closest I came to actually being knocked off was about an hour before I saw the dog get run over. I was riding towards a cow – which, as usual, was in the middle of the road. Unusually, this one didn't stand its ground. Instead, it gave itself a huge fright and scampered off. This would have been fine, but it just so happened that the cow was tied to a tree on the side of the road. Unaware of this, the cow carried on running in what it thought was a straight line. It ended up doing a full loop around the tree trunk and ran back into the road, coming within centimetres of the object it was running away from – me.

BIRDS

There were a few times, across all continents, where birds took a dislike to me. I'd hear them first, look up and find them circling my head until I left what I assume was their territory. Although, a couple of times in the US, I had to duck to avoid one diving at my head.

However, the most notable ornithological experience was with an emu on Day 80:

The highlight of the day came when an emu decided it wanted a race. There I was, cycling along, minding my own business, and, after hearing something in the bushes, I looked to my right, to see an emu running alongside me. I'm not entirely sure what it was doing, but it stayed with me for about a minute, and it seemed to be in a bit of a hurry. I must say, I was impressed by how fast it was. So, a word of warning: if an emu ever decides to chase you and you don't have a bike or a car – you're in trouble.

When it happened, I got my phone out to film it. Unfortunately, I forgot to press the record button, so ended up not getting any footage.

MONKEYS

Day 71 – Malaysia

I cycled past a lot of monkeys today, and most of them simply looked at me with astonishment. An expression very similar to what I got in India. I must say, I found it pretty amazing how human their reactions were (the monkeys that is).

However, there was one who went a bit mental; maybe he took offence at my hairless legs – I'm not sure. Regardless, he gave me the fright of my life when he started screaming and chasing me. I was instantly pulled from wherever my attention had wandered off to, and I think my heart rate hit a new high for this trip.

I went into a full-on sprint to out-run that one.

KOALAS

Koalas didn't pose any problems at all. In fact, I saw very few of them, and my only noteworthy experience was on my day off in Bairnsdale. I feel they deserve a special mention though, simply because I find it hilarious that they spend all their time 'tripping' from eucalyptus leaves. Wombats are cool too. I only saw one of them, and it was dead, but I hadn't realised how big they can be. They are definitely amongst the sturdiest creatures out there. I'm not sure what managed to kill the one I saw, but I'm guessing it had to be a truck.

INDIA:
PART 1

India is a different world. It's the kind of place that really cannot be totally described through words, pictures or even film. Experiencing the country first-hand is something I will always be grateful for, and, in my view, the only way to fully appreciate what the country is truly like.

After getting off the plane and making my way to passport control in Mumbai airport, I found myself in a large group of people, almost none of whom knew what was going on. The few tourists amongst them were all looking to each other for help, and the rest of the people were coming up with their own novel ways to queue and conduct themselves in a crowd.

Indian culture is different to what I have grown up with in London, in almost every single aspect of life; so, if I ever criticise the way things are done, please do not mistake my ignorance for insult. I am merely bemused by everything; nothing I say should be taken too seriously. In fact, that's a good rule to apply to everything I write – particularly when it comes to my experiences in the US.

Immigration forms only made the whole process more complicated. For some unknown reason, they didn't give the forms out on the plane – I can only assume they decided that would be far too efficient. Instead, all tourists had to fill them out in a small room, once inside the terminal. The problem was that the locals returning home (of which there were many) didn't know they were not required to fill one out, and, to be extra helpful, all the signs stating this were written in English. In short, the result was hundreds of passengers scrabbling over a handful of pens, in a room that can only be described as a large corridor. After that experience, I memorised my passport number and made sure I had a pen to hand for every flight I took.

Whilst in Mumbai, I was looked after by Fereshte. She was a friend of a friend, and, out of unparalleled generosity, had offered to keep me alive and help me adjust to India over the 48 hours before I started riding.

I fell in love (unfortunately, not permanently) with India as soon as I stepped out of the airport. It was 6am, but the heat hit me straight away, and after riding through snow for the past month I couldn't help but smile.

I was met by Fereshte's driver who would take me to her apartment. Without thinking anything of it, I got in the front passenger seat next to him and proceeded to ask questions about everything we passed. He only spoke very limited English, and, to his credit, I didn't realise this until 15 minutes into the journey, when it dawned on me that he wasn't just being shy. It also hadn't occurred to me that sitting in the front seat was unusual, and I was expected to sit in the back.

Those first couple of days were incredible, and I spent much of them committing numerous cultural faux pas. Just in the car journey alone, there were several that I soon became aware of.

These included loading my own bags into the car, wearing a seatbelt and assuming we would have to stop at red lights.

Upon being greeted and shown to my room in Fereshte's apartment, I headed to bed for a short nap. I hadn't slept on the plane, so jet lag was inevitably going to hit me if I didn't have a rest. Fortunately, life in India tends not to begin until around 9am, so I had a couple of hours spare. Fereshte was at work, but had made sure that her driver was on call to take me there whenever I was ready.

My first nap was uncomfortably hot. Naturally, I slept in nothing but boxers, something fairly common in the Western world, especially when it's so warm. Unfortunately, this gave the cleaning maid a shock when she walked in on me. That sleep taught me two things: dress modestly and don't forget to use the air-conditioning. At least I was learning.

The majority of the day was spent exploring the city. I was taken around by either Fereshte or Mosin, her assistant, to see some of the many sights and sample the different foods. This was important, as, arriving in India, I had no idea what I would be able to eat throughout the stint. The quality of food I ate in Mumbai was significantly higher than what I was able to find in the villages I would later ride through. Consequently, I would say that India is worth visiting for the food alone, as long as you get it in the right place.

Much of the second day was spent preparing for departure the following morning. This included rebuilding my bike, which became particularly stressful when I lost a couple of screws during the process. I was loving India, but didn't have a clue how I was going to survive once on the road. I didn't know where I would stay, where to get food and water, or what the roads would be like. I didn't know if covering 100 miles a day would even be remotely possible. I was also concerned that I would do something wrong from a cultural point of view, so I put a lot of pressure on myself to learn as much as possible during those two days in Mumbai.

Once most of the bike admin had been taken care of, Mosin took me out in the city to show me more. I should probably say once again at this point that I am an awful tourist. I like seeing the sights of the places I visit, but I'm quite happy seeing them and moving on after a minute or two. This isn't always the case, but I wouldn't say I'm the type to wander round museums for hours. The fact that I left Mumbai feeling as though I could have spent another few days simply being shown around the city goes to show how extraordinary it is. Yes, there are downsides – the hygiene in India isn't great and the driving is even worse – but everything is so unbelievably different from what I had grown up with that I was constantly amazed by it all.

My final dinner in the city was a very tasty affair and marked the end of my time in Mumbai, as I was leaving the next morning. As well as being an incredible experience, the two days had been crucial for helping me adapt to the country. I was still terrified by what lay ahead, but I was aching to get going and start clocking up the miles.

I was introduced to a friend of Fereshte at dinner, who was fairly sure that I would not be able to hit 100 miles a day in India. All credit to him, he was still supportive of my target and offered an amazing amount of assistance. Throughout the following two weeks, he insisted I call him every evening, so he could check I was okay and staying somewhere safe. I didn't mind that he didn't think I could do what I planned. Partly because, before setting off from Mumbai, I wasn't sure if I would be able to prove him wrong, but mainly because of the way he approached it. He wasn't being negative, he didn't patronise me and he still encouraged me to try to do it. Before I left London there were only three people who told me I wouldn't be able to do what I had planned, but all of them spoke to me in the same condescending tone. Oddly, their thoughts never actually bothered me though; I just ignored them and moved on.

I started my Indian leg just south of the city, after catching a ferry across the bay, to avoid riding through hours of Mumbai traffic. The ferry in itself was an experience. I didn't have a clue what was going on or where I was meant to be, but Fereshte was on hand to make sure I got on the right boat. I was still new to Indian custom, and had she not been there, I would have politely queued until the boat left. Standing back and waiting your turn doesn't get you very far in India.

Once on the ferry, I sat next to a well-travelled local. He spoke decent English, and had been to both Paris and London on more than one occasion. He quizzed me for the entire crossing, and – whilst I found it a bit draining at the time – in hindsight, it was actually a gentle introduction into what I would experience over the following weeks.

It was already 10am by the time I'd got off the ferry and started cycling. With the later start, and because I knew nothing about what was ahead of me, I was planning to stop for the day in a town that was only 60 miles down the road. I also wanted to finish earlier so that I could get more of a bearing on my new surroundings and what would have to be a new evening routine.

The first couple of hours were brilliant: I was flying along and loving the warm weather. The road deteriorated in places though (predictably), and I ended up getting a puncture. From there, my mood fluctuated, and I am currently feeling a bit stressed. This leg could be very hard or it could be amazing; I had a bit of both today.

On the brighter side, I had thousands of people say hello to me, and there were a number of very good views. It also happens to be a national holiday (I think), and a couple of guys invited me to a game of cricket, whilst driving along next to me. I declined, but it was a very nice gesture. I think they probably just wanted a laugh.

I had managed to make it to 80 miles – 20 more than planned. This was despite the puncture and struggling with the heat later on in the day. When I arrived at my revised target of Mangaon, the streets were filled with people having a party, and it took me a while to find somewhere to stay for the night. It's weird, outside of the big cities, restaurants write *"hotel"* on their signs. I found this extremely misleading and it took me a couple of days to realise I needed to look out for the word *"lodge"* if I wanted a place to sleep.

I eventually found somewhere that turned out to be unexpectedly adequate – minus toilet paper. When I asked the guy at the front desk if I could have some, it hadn't even occurred to me that this was an unusual request, but he went to the shops and returned five minutes later having bought some.

Not only was I acting oddly to these people, I also looked an absolute state. I hadn't noticed until I looked in the mirror, but my face was caked in dirt, and my white T-shirt was already brown.

Dinner was okay. The food I received served a purpose, but it was nothing compared to what I had been treated to in Mumbai. A chubby kid sitting opposite me laughed hysterically at my attempts to order in extremely limited Hindi. Moments like that quickly made me realise that being self-conscious would get me nowhere.

After dinner, I started preparing myself for the next day. I was planning to leave at 7am to get a few hours' riding done before the main heat of the day. This meant I had to sort out my breakfast the evening before, so I bought a couple of packets of biscuits.

I got a bit stressed after that. The feeling stemmed from a combination of trying and failing to fix my punctured inner tube, and not knowing a single thing about life in India. It dawned on me that I was in a pretty ridiculous situation, and was improvising my way through it. If punctures were to be a daily occurrence, I was going to struggle, and probably run out of repair patches (thankfully, that didn't happen).

The next day went something like this:

After a breakfast consisting of biscuits, I set off around 7am and was pleasantly surprised to find it below 20°C. The day was due to be just under 100 miles, but with a fair bit of climbing, so I was expecting to finish around 5pm. However, by accident, I rode past the town I had planned to stop in, and only realised my mistake after a further five kilometres. I then set the finishing point for the next opportunity, another 25 kilometres up the road.

The first few hours were great: my speed was good, the scenery was interesting, and I was eating and drinking better than yesterday. Only a handful of roads were in need of maintenance, so, thankfully, no punctures today either.

The day only got hard around 2pm when the heat got to me. I was heading up what I thought was the final big climb of the day (the extra miles added one more), when the temperature rose to over 40°C. With no breeze, I really started to feel it. At the top, I had to take a half-hour break to recover. I reckon I got a bit dehydrated at this point, because an hour later I had to stop to recover again. Feeling very light-headed, I sat on the roadside drinking as much as I could. Slowly, I improved, and, for the last half-hour of the ride, I started to feel good again.

Unfortunately, missing my stop added an extra hour of riding. Ordinarily, this would not be the biggest issue, but, at the time, my stomach was feeling extremely unsettled. I won't go into detail, and, although I didn't quite need to rush into the bushes, it made the final part of the ride a bit uncomfortable. Finishing the day with a climb did not help the situation either.

When I arrived at the next town, the heat had drained me, and I was desperate to find somewhere to stop for the night. I ended up paying far too much for what was an extremely unpleasant room. Haggling was not something I ever mastered. The only time I ever spent any money was on food or accommodation. With the food, I tended to stick to packaged food (on the advice of Fereshte) during the day, and this always had prices on it, so it was difficult to argue for any less. Furthermore, the prices for this kind of thing were so low compared to England anyway. As for the 'hotel' rooms, this was generally something that had to be sorted out at the end of the day. I'd arrive tired, and it would be immediately apparent that I was not going to carry on to the next town, so really I had nothing to bargain with. On top of this, the room prices would often be written down, so, again, I felt I didn't have any real basis on which to haggle.

That second evening in India was a different matter; I definitely should have haggled because the guy behind the front desk took me to the cleaners. I paid about four times what I should have done, but this didn't occur to me until I'd already been to the toilet, by which point I wasn't really in a position to ask for a refund.

Dinner that night was also shocking, and demonstrated why so many Indians are vegetarians. I had eaten vegetarian the night before, so this was my first experience of meat in rural India. I believe I ordered a chicken tikka masala, but it was very different to the English version. The chicken was more bone than meat, and the 'meat' that there was, was far from appetising. The sauce was also nothing like the creamy one you'd expect in a typical Indian restaurant back home. There was no flavour, an off-putting texture and, for all intents and purposes, it may as well have been fire.

Going into this trip, I was about average when it came to handling spicy food. I could put up with a reasonable level of spice, but I didn't ever see the appeal of it. I never understood why you would make something so spicy that it masks the flavours. When I got to India, I realised that, in a lot of cases, burning your tongue off is more desirable than tasting what you're eating. I would generally get through three milkshakes per meal if I ordered a curry whilst in India. I'm sure the locals took great amusement in watching the silly white boy sweat his entire face off. Needless to say, on a regular basis, I would instantly regret ordering whatever arrived in front of me.

By the end of my India leg, I had developed a hatred of spicy food. However, when I met my family in Thailand, that changed. It wasn't until I joined them that I noticed I had built up a tolerance over the previous month. Before I left the UK, I would never enjoy whatever curry my dad might have ordered, but, after struggling through so many spicy meals in India, I found myself enjoying food that was giving him trouble. My 'spice tolerance' is returning to normal now, but for a good year after the trip, I completely understood why some people actually like spicy food.

Day 3 in India was more of the same – barely surviving the traffic and the heat, marvelling at the culture, and revelling in the generosity of the locals:

I also encountered some more very friendly people. At the top of one of the climbs, there was a little shrine where I sat down to recover. A group of people showed up, and, once they'd finished praying, they started talking to me. They were extremely interested in my trip and even asked for a photo with me. I can't remember if I mentioned that this happened on the first day as well, but, either way, that's the second photo I've given. Maybe I should start charging people.

After they left, the guy who was sitting/working/living in the shrine came over and offered me a couple of bananas – obviously it was clear I was suffering. I don't think there is anything that would've made me happier at that point. Once I'd eaten them both, he came over again and gave me two more. I've learnt from a rather messy incident in Albania, that putting bananas in my bag is a bad idea. Because of this, I ate those two as well and I must admit – even for me – four bananas in one sitting is a bit excessive, and they did take a while to go down. However iffy I felt though, I was in a very good mood. I've been craving a banana (not a euphemism) for about a week, and that had me smiling for the rest of the ride. So, to the old fellow on the hill, if you're listening, thank you very much – you made my day.

For Day 4 in India, I'm going to refer entirely to my blog as, for once, I did a reasonable job of covering everything that day:

Today has mostly been a good day. The owner of the hotel got up especially early in order to provide me with breakfast (for free as well). It wasn't huge, but it filled a hole, and the generosity put me in a good mood.

The morning was fast. The temperature was below 25°C and the terrain was flat as well, meaning I knocked off the first 60 kilometres easily.

There were a couple of climbs in the second half of the day, but nothing major, so the heat didn't affect me quite as badly as it has done the last two days. Although I am a bit sunburnt in places.

I hit Goa today, which was good. Cycling through the state capital Panjim was busy, but I found a place to stop for a decent lunch. It was called Biryani & More. Although – surprise, surprise – the word 'more' was a lie, as they actually only served biryanis. It was, however, very tasty, so I didn't mind.

I've eaten quite well today and also treated myself to a few milkshakes: sweet lime, pineapple, banana (x2) and Oreo. It seems juices and the like are very popular in India, and I can see why! I sampled a fair few in Mumbai as well.

Up to the five-hour mark, the ride was fantastic. Unfortunately, it went slightly downhill after that. A headwind picked up out of nowhere. It wasn't as bad as in Europe, but it was enough to annoy me. The road also went bad for about 500m, and, in that time, a screw on my pannier rack fell out. By the time

I noticed, it was too late to go back, and this caused a pretty severe sense of humour failure. I started getting annoyed at anyone who beeped at me. This wouldn't necessarily be a problem in England, but here it meant I was constantly muttering abuse at strangers. I have now been to work with some zip ties, so all should be well. [As it turned out, all was not well. The zip ties broke very early on the next day and I had to improvise further with some wire I found on the roadside.]

Thankfully, Goa isn't actually too bad. I've been down to the beach for a swim, and I'm now feeling much better about everything. I'm currently pondering the meaning of the Indian head wiggle. After reviewing my experiences, I think I've managed to narrow it down to five options:

- *Yes*
- *No*
- *I have no idea what you're saying*
- *Of course it's spicy*
- *What's wrong with our tap water?*

Any help on this matter would be gratefully received.

Goa was interesting. It's the place I had heard the most about before setting off from Mumbai, both from the Brits and the locals. From what I gather, it's very much a holiday destination, and it's a popular long-weekend destination for those based in Mumbai. I had been told I should definitely take a couple of days off there (although that was mostly by those who didn't understand what I was doing).

I ended up not being that keen on Goa. Panjim – the state capital – seemed really nice, but I only stopped there briefly for some food. I stayed in a place called Benaulim, and it was the only place in India that, as a white guy, I didn't feel like I was in a minority. Take from that what you will, but I felt it lacked the culture and the charm that amazed me throughout the rest of the country.

The beaches I saw were stunning, but that was the case in many other places, and it was far more crowded than in Karnataka – the next state down the coast. As for the party scene that Goa is famous for, I didn't see any of that, so perhaps I'm missing the whole point.

I began to settle into a rhythm after that, and the remaining six and a half days to Kanyakumari were somewhat repetitive. Unlike Europe though, this did not lead to boredom, as there was still lots to look at. Kanyakumari is the southernmost point of India, and was therefore where I stopped riding south-east down the west coast, and started riding north-east up the east coast.

During that week between Goa and Kanyakumari, I fell in love with India. I remained completely out of my depth, but managed to find some form of routine and allowed myself to relax a little. The driving was an exception to this rule. After leaving Goa, I became increasingly frustrated at the ineptitude of those I was sharing the road with, until I completely lost my cool three days later.

Gaining some sense of routine was imperative to being able to relax and explore in the evenings. I was able to briefly look around a couple of temples in Murudeshwar and Tirchendur. The former is home to the second largest statue of Shiva (a Hindu god) in the world.

It was also during that second week that I began to fully appreciate the extent of Indian hospitality. Something that deserves an entire chapter to itself, along with my full thoughts and experiences of Indian traffic. Most importantly of all, Day 35 (so five days after leaving Goa) marked a very momentous occasion in my life as a cyclist…

HAIR(LESS)

As I am sure most of you know, male cyclists are (in)famous for shaving their legs. A fact that confuses the masses and makes many sceptical of their masculinity.

I'll start with the reasons why, because I know that's what most of the normal people reading this will be wondering.

There are a number of reasons, varying in levels of legitimacy. The first potential argument is aerodynamics, and, whilst some studies claim that it can make a difference, any gains to be had are going to be minimal. Justifiable perhaps, if you're going for Olympic gold.

Another reason that gets batted around is that shaven legs make it easier for masseurs to apply oils (massages can help recovery). Again, if you're getting massages every day for performance reasons, and you are not a professional, you had better have deep pockets or be attempting something pretty extreme.

One of the more reasonable excuses is that it makes it far easier to clean wounds after crashes. This is the one I usually lead with when put on the spot, and I have even had a nurse confirm this notion for me when she was scraping some gravel out of my leg. Unfortunately, crashing often features in bike racing, and, unless you want an infection, there is nothing more effective than giving your cuts a good scrub. Having hair makes the whole procedure more difficult.

Lastly, and probably the honest reason why most cyclists shave their legs – tradition. It's just the way things are done. Why is this the case? Who knows? It could be a combination of the above reasons, or perhaps an eccentric Italian pro one day decided it looked better and convinced some others to do the same.

On that note, it does look better. Granted, that statement does not apply to normal life, but, when clad in Lycra, hairless legs are the way to go. Not to mention that it makes the cultivation of tan lines far easier – more on that later.

I haven't always shaved my legs. I didn't when I started cycling aged 15, and I still didn't when I set off around the world aged 19. I previously thought that shaved legs should be reserved for racers and people who were fast enough to justify doing something so socially unacceptable. I didn't feel that I fell into this bracket, and I certainly didn't think the consequences of sporting hairless legs in a student rugby match outweighed the benefits. I do shave my legs now, and I have slightly altered my views. I feel that anyone can do what they like with their leg hair, even if you're not a cyclist, although that might be even more questionable.

I first shaved my legs in India, on Day 35. Initially, I did it out of necessity and with a great deal of apprehension. After each day of riding in India, my body and clothes would be covered in dirt, and each evening I would spend ages cleaning both. This became even more laborious when a small tap was all I had at my disposal. With leg hair, cleaning the grime off was a nightmare and it took a lot of vigorous scrubbing to get them even vaguely clean. After I shaved them (a decision I went back and forth on for a few days), the dirt ran straight off, saving both time and energy.

The shaving itself took bloody ages. I had a £7 pair of clippers and a single-bladed razor to go to work with, and I almost gave up half way through to go for dinner.

Having since left the Indian countryside and returned to Britain, I no longer face the same issues of dirt roads and dysfunctional showers, so my initial and genuine excuse for needing smooth legs is no longer valid. Nowadays, I shave my legs based on the other aforementioned reasons and a misplaced pride in being a 'cyclist'. If you also ride a bike often, and are on the fence about the whole thing, go for it – you'll feel faster and it's a good conversation starter in normal situations; the difficulty is keeping the conversation going after you've exhausted that topic.

RULES OF THE ROADS

When I reached Australia, I was often told by people to be careful on the roads because the drivers were the worst in the world. The same was true of the US. It wasn't just British ex-pats who said this either, it was often the locals who would warn me. I appreciated the warnings, but trust me when I say, if you live somewhere that is not India you do not have the worst drivers on the planet – not even close. Admittedly, I've not been to Africa or Russia, so I can't say that with 100% certainty, but India would take some beating.

I have grown up cycling in a city of over 8 million people, and have therefore encountered a lot of morons on the road. Having now covered a range of countries, I wouldn't say that the US or Australia is any worse than London – I can deal with the occasional didgeridoo-toting maniac. India on the other hand is in a completely different league.

Before arriving in Mumbai, I had already come across fairly lax driving laws in the likes of Albania and Turkey, even in Greece, where they deem it acceptable to double-park wherever they want, as long as they have their hazard lights on.

India is unique, and I am sure you could write a short book on the ins and outs of the traffic there. I'm not going to do that, but I will write a brief chapter on my experiences. Firstly, some advice: do not ride a bike across/through the country – that would be a stupid thing to do.

I'm being serious. If someone had said that to me before I set off, I would have ignored them. Just like if you already have your mind set on cycle touring through India, you will ignore my advice. However, if you are in two minds about the whole thing because it could be a bit dangerous, don't do it. Get a driver or do it on foot.

Taking a ferry out of Mumbai on my first day was a good idea, because, without first adjusting to the traffic on some quieter country roads, I most likely would have died. When I arrived in India, Fereshte's brother asked me (sincerely), which side of the road I cycle on. I thought he was joking, but he followed it up with the statement, "I like to see what's coming." He then suggested I consider riding on the wrong side of the road myself. That set the tone for the coming weeks, as I discovered it was not only some cyclists that took this option, but all manner of vehicles, including trucks.

Whilst staying in Mumbai, I learnt a few crucial things about Indian traffic laws. Firstly, as already mentioned, traffic lights are nothing more than decoration and should be ignored. Secondly, the horn should be used as often as possible. It can mean anything from "Get out of my way" or "I'm overtaking", to "You look funny, fancy a chat?"

As I headed down the west coast, I felt the traffic was getting worse and worse. Whether that was the case or just that my patience had started to wear thin, I'm not sure. I started to see more *extremely* risky overtakes, and came across more vehicles that had clearly misjudged their manoeuvres.

A word on the overtaking. India is a developing country, and so there is a large range of vehicles on the road: from 40-year-old trucks that struggled to move faster than me to modern-day cars. This creates a huge difference in speed capabilities amongst the vehicles, which are often sharing only a single lane, so there is bound to be a need to overtake. The problems arise when the drivers decide to overtake each other regardless of whether something is coming the other way. Indian drivers don't look, they seem to live by the motto "Pull out, and hope for the best." Not something I would advise in any endeavour…

As for the constant beeping, this really wore me down, especially if I was in a bad mood or feeling tired – which was often the case. My patience ran out on Day 33 (Day 7 in India). Over the preceding few days, I'd had to venture off-road on a number of occasions to avoid becoming a mixture of ex-human and ex-bike. When I hit Kannur, towards the end of Day 33, I was already irritable. My Garmin had taken me the wrong way, and I had wasted 40 minutes dicking around on the wrong roads. That evening I wrote the following in my blog:

> *Had I written this a few hours ago, it would've been me hurling abuse at the Indian drivers for multiple pages. I have since calmed down a bit, so I'll restrict it to a paragraph.*
>
> *It was the last bit of the day that was a pain – cycling through Kannur (which is quite a big place). I genuinely can't get my head round the driving here – how that many people can think it's acceptable to drive like they do just baffles me. I think there was more common sense in the Year 3 class I taught in the autumn than in all the drivers in that town. I also can't figure out who (if anyone) has right of way at roundabouts. It pretty much comes down to a game of chicken. This – when you know that's the case – isn't so*

bad, although I'm yet to win against a truck. The fact that I was constantly looking out for idiotic cars meant I wasn't looking at my GPS and ended up going the wrong way. This tipped me over the edge and caused a bit of road rage. To be fair to myself, I'm not sure it was road rage, it was more like I've-nearly-died-a-million-times rage, and probably quite justified.

I finally made it out, and the last 10 kilometres were actually not too bad. A lot of anger went into my pedals for that stretch, so it passed quite quickly.

After that release of frustration, things got better. Not the drivers, they were still terrible, but I got better at dealing with them. I stopped trying to fight the broken system and decided to join it. The post I wrote the following day was significantly more upbeat:

At one point I cycled through Kozhikode – another fairly big place – and, as expected, the traffic was manic. Luckily, I'd had a change of heart and I really enjoyed riding through it. I've come to realise over the last week that, in order to survive an Indian road, you must drive (or ride) like an Indian. I didn't quite go that far, but I did stop riding as I would in England (or any sane country for that matter). In case you come to India and rent a car, I feel I should elaborate on this piece of advice:

– DO NOT copy them when they stop in the middle of the road, pull out without looking, drive on the wrong side of the road or do a U-turn in a tuk-tuk (they have the worst turning circle of any vehicle ever invented).

- DO make noise at everything (if you have a horn use that, otherwise shout), ignore the existence of lane markings, assume you have right of way even when you don't (sounds like a bad idea, but you'll get nowhere if you let braver / more stupid people in front of you).

That is essentially my advice on managing the traffic in India. I somehow made it through without crashing. I came close a couple of times, and I did have one minor incident whilst waiting at some traffic lights. A guy on a motorbike accidently released his clutch and drove into me. Thankfully, the bike and I were both fine.

I could never recommend riding a bike in India with a clear conscience. The best alternative would be to hire a moped, so long as you're a competent rider, and enjoy an adrenaline hit. If you drive a car instead and have to venture into a town, you will hit something – or, more accurately, something will hit you – so get a driver. Otherwise, taxis and tuk-tuks should suffice in most situations.

One final thing to mention: beware of festivals. Towards the end of Day 34, I found the road blocked by 10 elephants and lots of brightly coloured Indians. It took about 15 minutes to walk my bike through the festivities – I have no idea what all the other traffic did.

I could go on. I could tell you about the numerous people who encouraged me to hold on to their vehicles, or how I was once threatened with a crowbar by someone who mistakenly thought I was holding on to his vehicle. However, for now I will leave it there. Hopefully, this brief insight will help some of you to stay alive.

INDIAN HOSPITALITY

Whilst I was in a constant state of bewildered awe in India, the locals all found me and my complexion just as fascinating, judging by the reactions I received. I was a novelty, and I was reminded of that everywhere I went. Whenever I rode by, the people would literally stop what they were doing and stare, mouth agape. Their reactions were comical, but, in a place where subtlety is unnecessary, I would expect nothing less. Every time I stopped for a rest and something to eat, a crowd of people would gather around me. Those who spoke English would ask me countless questions, and those who didn't seemed content to just watch me. I felt like an animal in a zoo to start with, and I wasn't overly comfortable with the whole thing. But, by the end of the four weeks, any insecurities I may have had were gone.

On my final riding day in India, I stopped in a town to get some food. I attracted a group of about 20 people, but couldn't find anywhere to sit. Instead, I sat on the ground eating my crisps with the huddle of locals standing in a semi-circle around me, all of them just staring. I felt like they were expecting me to start juggling or something; instead, I just smiled. After a while, one of them returned with a friend who spoke English, at which point they all bombarded him with questions to ask me. Fun.

The unrelenting attention I received was ultimately what wore me down. Over time, I struggled with the lack of peace and quiet, but I think it would be unfair to hold that against the country. Hospitality in India is unparalleled. Everyone goes out of their way to help you, and the constant questions come from a genuine interest. When I stopped briefly in Kanyakumari, the southernmost point, I felt like more of an attraction than the coastline. I only stopped for 10 minutes, but, in that time, seven people took photos with me and one asked for my autograph. I don't know why he wanted my signature, but it turned out he didn't have a pen, so he had to settle for a photo as well.

I always seemed to provide the most interest for people, despite India providing a constant source of crazy sights for me. The pinnacle of innovation: that's how I described the country when I happened across a man combing his hair with a toothbrush. Retrospectively, I'm not sure that 'innovative' is an appropriate description of India, but it is definitely unusual. I found the people there absolutely fascinating, and perhaps that's just it. I was as much of a novelty to them as they were to me. The absurdity of some things I witnessed never ceased to amaze me: in Chennai, I saw a man out for a morning jog, but running backwards; in Puducherry, I found a man with a pet elephant; in Chirala, I rode past someone herding about 500 ducks (on foot); and on Day 48 someone tried to buy my bike whilst I was riding it. I jokingly suggested I would swap it for the motorbike he was riding, but when he agreed I had to backtrack rapidly. I also once got offered a live fish in a plastic bag as a gift. For the life of me, I cannot remember why or how that came about. I also encountered a wonderful hotel owner who adorned me in flowers, and, on my first day, a passing local took it upon himself to pump up my tyre after I punctured.

The one thing I did not act on was an invitation for what I presume was tea. It was towards the end of the day, and my patience had already been worn out from the wind and the incessant questions, when I was invited to have a drink with a group of locals. I use 'invited' loosely in this case, mind you – I was riding through a town when a man shouted to me in Hindi as I passed. The intention was clear, but I feigned ignorance with a polite smile and carried on pedalling. I felt really bad about that. I was in a shite mood at the time, and desperate to get to my stop for the night, but I would change my mind if I was going through it again. I'd have been stuck there all through dinner, if not all night, but I felt guilty since the man was merely being friendly.

CITIES

I didn't necessarily try to avoid cities whilst riding, but I certainly didn't go searching for them. They were often a navigational nightmare and just slowed me down. Of the cities I did see, I still only stayed for a matter of hours in many cases.

I feel I should write a little summary of some of the cities I visited, but please feel free to ignore my thoughts. I'm simply sharing how I felt after hours in the saddle, and my advice would be to trust a more reputable travel guide. Furthermore, this is only a small sample of the cities I went to. If I've left one out, it is either because I have mentioned it elsewhere in this book or, more likely, because I didn't see enough to write anything interesting about it.

ISTANBUL

Istanbul was cool. I have briefly described my time there already, but here is a bit more. The traffic is nuts; I would not recommend cycling there. However, unlike India, if you rent a car yourself you should just about manage. The Grand Bazaar was closed when I looked round the city, but the Spice Bazaar was open and that was really interesting. Top tip: haggle for your Turkish delight or you will be severely ripped off.

The mosques (including the blue one) are great if you're interested in that kind of thing; I wasn't. My day was largely dictated by meals, with brief interludes of looking at stuff. I'm glad I have seen them, but I'm not rushing back.

I didn't go to the Asian side of the city, so I can't comment on that. I also went in winter, and it was absolutely freezing, so I didn't experience any of the sun that Istanbul is famous for.

The food was great; there were loads of new things to try, all of which were fantastic. I suppose it depends largely on where you buy it from, but it was definitely the highlight of the place for me.

Shisha isn't really my scene, so I can't comment on that either. Most places seemed to offer it though. Obviously, there is lots I missed out on, but I would definitely recommend a visit. Go when it's warm, and eat lots of the food.

MUMBAI AND KOLKATA

Mental. Absolutely fucking mental. I think that goes for the whole of India, but Mumbai was my first experience of the country, so it made a big impression on me. Kolkata was my final stop in India, and, by that point, I felt there was little I hadn't already seen. After three weeks, I had grown accustomed to the country, so I approached Kolkata with a very different mindset. My dad, who met me in Kolkata, had flown in from England, and I suspect his feelings mirrored mine in Mumbai.

My views of Kolkata were also swayed as I was desperate to move on by that point, so I won't say any more about it. Mumbai was incredible and well worth a visit. It encapsulated everything about India, and I can't sum it up in a short paragraph. There is a lot to see, and, once again, the food is incredible if you go to the right places. Approach with caution if you're a hygiene freak.

PUDUCHERRY

Formerly known as Pondicherry, this was my favourite place in India. It is next to the sea, and the French influence remains clear – even the road names are French. The houses are painted in bright colours, and the whole city feels attractive. Puducherry still has the typical Indian bustle, but is less manic and far more manageable than the likes of Mumbai or Kolkata. I was able to cross a couple of roads without fearing for my life, and even came across a perfectly house-trained elephant standing in the street.

I was only there for one afternoon, but if you travel to India from a long way away, you would be missing out if you didn't try to visit Puducherry.

MANDALAY

The drive from the airport is fairly uninspiring, but, once you get into the city, it's really quite nice. There's lots to see, and it's as yet unspoilt. When I went, it was quiet enough for anyone to ride around and explore on a bike. Avoid eating pig's ear though; there are much tastier things to try.

PERTH, ADELAIDE AND SYDNEY

I loved all the Australian cities I visited. I went to Brisbane as well, but I wasn't there for long. I missed out on Melbourne too, because I took a ferry to the south of the city.

Part of my fondness for the cities in Australia came down to the novelty of having stunning beaches outside the front door. This, and the laid-back attitude everyone appeared to have. There is a massive sporting culture, which I loved, and everybody seemed far more relaxed than somewhere like London.

I loved Sydney. I spent the day with my cousin in Manly, which is slightly out of the centre. A few of my friends have told me that public transport there is a nightmare, but I didn't have cause to discover that. What I would say is that Sydney is surprisingly hilly, and is not ideal if you are hoping to cycle between tourist attractions. Unless you are training, in which case it's great. (Manly is awesome, go there.)

SAN FRANCISCO

I stayed in Tiburon when I was there, thanks to the hospitality of another friend of the family, but I did venture into the city for half a day to explore. Getting a cab from the airport was unusually eventful. The people managing the queue were somewhat perplexed by my bike box and didn't know how to handle the situation. When I was eventually given a cab, I was met by an interesting driver. He had an unfortunate speech impediment that seemed to be directly proportional to his stress levels. It went into overdrive when I pointed out that he had driven five miles but forgotten to close the boot. That cab trip was the only time I went over the Golden Gate Bridge, but even whilst I was on it I could barely see the bloody thing because of the clouds. San Francisco really has a microclimate unto itself.

I saw a bit more of the bridge (as well as Alcatraz) when I took the ferry to the city the next day. I was on foot, so I couldn't cover much of it, but I went around most of the pier area and into the city centre to buy some swimming trunks. It's another (famously) hilly city with many street performers and artists. I was also asked openly if I wanted to buy any weed. I didn't, but it's the thought that counts. It's worth a visit, but do not be deceived by California's reputation for fantastic weather. San Francisco is more like London in that regard.

LONDON

After briefly sampling all these cities, I concluded that London is the best, by quite some margin. I fell in love with London whilst I was away. This is probably because it's my home town, but, by the time I reached North America, I couldn't wait to get back.

INDIA:
PART 2

Reaching Kanyakumari came just under halfway through Day 37. This meant I had 13 days of riding still to do before reaching Kolkata. I experienced a big shift in emotions towards the country during that time, but it was still a few days after leaving the southernmost point before my patience completely ran out:

The day changed almost instantly as I started heading up the east coast. The road became a bit worse for a start - it seems that they are doing a lot of work on it - so, for the remainder of the day, I frequently found myself riding over stretches of rubble or sand, neither of which are much fun. [This was followed by an entire paragraph moaning about a headwind.]

I stopped with 30 miles remaining at a small village. So far, there have been fewer places to stop between towns, so I did not have much choice. Here, I was cheered up by some local kids. I had absolutely no clue what they were saying, and they found it most amusing whenever I shrugged. They also enjoyed the novelty of a camera a lot.

After this, my mood improved. I still had to deal with the wind, but I was in a better place mentally. The last few days have been easy with the lack of wind and relatively high speeds. It's easier to let the mind wander. When the speed disappeared, I got frustrated, and it took a couple of hours for me to adjust and get over it. The rest of the ride was fairly enjoyable, albeit not fast.

With regards to where I am staying, it's pretty unique compared to the towns I have been in until now. It is home to another famous temple, and, apparently, it attracts thousands of people. There are hundreds sleeping on the streets around the town. At first, I was shocked, as I assumed it was just extreme poverty, but I have since realised that it is people who are visiting, and who are not able or willing to pay for a hotel. They're not homeless, they're just on holiday! It's really quite fascinating to see, but I guess they don't have to worry about rain as much as you would in England.

It's been an interesting evening, and the changes from the two coasts have been more dramatic than expected. I also ate my dinner off a banana leaf rather than a plate, which was a first.

A mixed day overall, but, since I have ridden the whole of the west coast of India from Mumbai, I guess it was pretty good!

The small group of children I met cheered me up massively. Not only that but their genuine happiness in the face of a significant amount of adversity made me realise I should stop being such a pussy. This feeling lasted for the rest of the ride, but, unfortunately, it did not carry over to the following day.

Dinner that evening was also an interesting affair. I was totally lost as to how to conduct myself, other than not using my left hand. I therefore resorted to copying the man in front of me. I was more than happy to eat my dinner with my fingers; the part I was sceptical about was the banana leaf itself. It had clearly already been used by someone else and all the gentleman opposite had done was to rinse it with water. Water that I wasn't supposed to drink. Thankfully, I did not get ill that night.

Day 38 was boring and windy (and therefore far from easy), so I won't dwell on it.

Day 39 was a change for the better, as I ticked off my first ride of more than 200 kilometres. It wasn't something I expected to do in India, but it boosted my confidence massively. I went into the day with a deliberately positive attitude. I forced myself to be upbeat, as I knew the extra 40 kilometres would play awful tricks with my mind if I didn't. I ended up riding for 75 kilometres before my first stop. It put me ahead of schedule, but I paid for it later on, and the last two hours of the day dragged.

The other significance of Day 39 was that it marked the final day of wearing the same T-shirt. When I set off from Mumbai I wore a white T-shirt instead of Lycra. Even by the end of that first day, the T-shirt was destined for the bin. I couldn't believe how filthy it had become so quickly. But, naturally, I decided to wear it the following day as well.

After a week of wearing it, I thought that I could potentially do all of India in the same T-shirt, which I thought would be pretty cool. A couple of days later, a local commented on how dirty I looked. Bearing in mind that cleanliness is not as prominent in India as in most other places, this made me realise that what I was doing was perhaps not that acceptable after all. My parents had organised a decent hotel for me at the end of Day 40, and, not wanting to turn up looking like Stig of the Dump, I opted for different attire that morning.

I wrote a post on my Facebook page to summarise its journey:

Yesterday turned out to be an even bigger occasion than I thought. It ended up being the final day of wearing the same T-shirt. Had I not completely lost track of the days, I probably would've worn it today, just to make it up to two weeks, but oh well.

I must admit, I've grown quite attached to it, so rather than throw it away, it has in fact carried on the journey with me. I'm sure many of you wanted me to see it all the way through, so I can only apologise. Pulling on a clean jersey this morning was extremely pleasant, and it's probably also worth mentioning that a white T-shirt can go slightly see-through. So, in addition to the tan lines on my legs, wrists, arms, fingers and ankles, I was on the brink of developing some very odd-looking ones on my back.

Final T-shirt statistics:
  Distance worn – 2,306 kilometres
  Sweat absorbed – 4 million litres
  Dirt collected – 1.2 tonnes
  Smell – questionable

The T-shirt in question is now in my wardrobe in London. Whilst it has been washed at least once, it is far from its original shade of white.

Day 40 was my favourite in India, and one of the best of the whole trip. The ride itself was good, but it was the afternoon in Puducherry that I really enjoyed:

Despite a breakfast of just biscuits, I set off in a good mood, aiming for an early finish. I had a decent hotel lined up, courtesy of my parents, and was eager to get there as soon as possible.

There was little wind to start with, and I made very good progress. I ate on the bike (more biscuits and crisps) and cycled through instead of stopping as normal. I hit some bad traffic at one point, but, other than that, the first two hours went by easily. I was aiming to stop at 60 kilometres for the first break, but a brother and sister on a motorbike were most interested in me, and I ended up going past that distance whilst talking to them [she was definitely flirting with me]. By the time they headed onwards, I was approaching 65 kilometres, and I thought that I might as well cycle until I reached 70 kilometres, as I was still feeling good. The two of them were very friendly, although I have noticed that a lot of Indians have great difficulty pronouncing my name. Seriously? I don't think it could be any simpler, but the most common one I get is "Som".

The ride was fairly similar all day. The wind kept changing, but was more or less in my favour. I only stopped twice and pedalled quickly, making today my earliest finish and a very good ride. The only downsides were leaving my credit card at last night's hotel and the fact that a rash has formed where my gym shorts overlap my cycling shorts. It's not painful, but it is something I could do without!

Since arriving at the hotel I have had a brilliant and extremely relaxing afternoon, although, as usual, I have left it too late to write this and I am absolutely knackered. To put this into context, I actually just turned down an offer to go for a drink with two Indian girls. Probably not my smartest move, but I am genuinely about to pass out.

Quick summary of this afternoon: I showered, explored Puducherry a bit (which is quite nice), saw an elephant, had a pizza, went for a swim and had dinner.

Oh, and for dinner, I had beef. I was more than a bit surprised to see it on the menu, and thought that it would be insane to miss the opportunity. A cow nearly ran into me today and almost caused some very dirty cycling shorts, so I just see it as revenge.

I really liked Puducherry, and I have already mentioned this, but I thoroughly recommend visiting. The following day was also a good one as I was still running on the highs of that afternoon.

After Day 41 I remember having 888 miles left to do in India, and setting my sights on finishing the whole leg within eight days. Once I had that target in my mind, my fuse instantly ran out. The final week in India is when it all changed, and, regrettably, I started to dislike the country.

I'm going to rely heavily on my blog for the next few days, as I think I did quite a good job of documenting my downward spiral into cultural intolerance.

Day 42 – Chennai to Nellore

After a fairly good breakfast, I headed out early in the hope that I would beat the traffic when riding through Chennai. I probably did, but an Indian city is an Indian city, and the drivers are still crazy. In case anyone is thinking of going there, here's my brief travel guide: some brilliant architecture, a couple of nice beaches, but, away from that area, it's not all that great.

Having not looked at the route last night, I was surprised at how big Chennai was. Riding through a city is slow, but the constant need for attention means that your mind is on other things and the miles ticked by nicely.

At one point, a tuk-tuk driver came up beside me and told me to hold on. Now this, I think, would be cheating, so I declined. Plus, any health-and-safety people reading this would have a fit. I felt a bit rude turning him down though, so I dipped into his slipstream for a while. It took him a minute to realise what was going on, but when he noticed I could keep up, he instantly got carried away with the speed. It was a fast but difficult couple of kilometres. When I dropped off, he came back and offered me a poppadom from a bucketful in the footwell. It was a bit stale, but the gesture was really appreciated.

Upon arriving at my destination – very early considering the distance – the day took a downhill slant, and I am now not really feeling that great, which is down to a combination of incompetent city planners, incompetent 'hotel' staff and credit-card issues.

Day 43 – Nellore to Chirala

My mood hasn't improved since yesterday evening, unfortunately. I got very little sleep and at one point woke up to find I had been feasted on by mosquitoes. Breakfast consisted of a cold bowl of rice I'd ordered the night before, so that was particularly uninspiring.

I was tired most of the day, but had a slight tailwind for the first couple of hours, which helped.

Not much happened until the last 50 kilometres. Apart from the early helping hand, the wind hadn't featured until then. It obviously decided that I'd had it too easy with the flat roads and that a headwind would be perfect. This did not do my mood any favours. All day I've been tired, and I'm also feeling the effects of the constant attention. When I do stop for something to eat, it's nice to have a bit of a rest, but often either me or my bike attract a lot of inquisitive locals, and I end up leaving even more stressed and weary. This wouldn't be so bad if it wasn't always exactly the same questions. I think I've been asked where I'm from at least 30 times a day since setting off from Mumbai.

Anyway, when the headwind hit, I was also joined by a man on a motorbike, who was even more interested than normal. One problem with having the wind in your face is that it's really difficult to hear, and it became a bit of an effort when I kept having to ask him to repeat himself. Especially as all I really wanted was to get my head down. After asking all the generic questions I'd come to expect, he asked me if I spoke Hindi and if I knew the Indian national anthem. I'd have thought it was clear that I did not. Anyway, after telling him that I didn't, he proceeded to try and teach me it line by line. This did not last long. Funnily enough, the wind instantly became too loud to even attempt to understand him...

Since arriving at my hotel, I've met a very enthusiastic man in charge, who's written to the local press and even planned out my trip for when I return with a fiancé in five years' time. I've got to make sure I'm here between the 13th and 16th January, so that he can take me to his local town and watch the cock fighting.

In other news, my hands hurt all day and I think I've developed a blister, which is annoying. Although, having said that, it could well be another mosquito bite. Worse still, I've just stubbed my toe extremely hard and it hurts like buggery. India is starting to hit back, and I sense that this final week could be a bit of a grind. I'd love to be wrong about that.

Day 44 – Chirala to Bhimavaram

I started off a bit later than I have been recently because of a few more photos with the hotel manager. This time he put on his 'formal dress' and gave me a floral necklace/wreath arrangement, which – after the photos – he wrapped around my handlebars and told me it would bring me good luck. I ditched it fairly promptly, but, as always, it was a very nice gesture.

Yesterday, I mentioned that I am asked where I am from about 30 times a day. I'll admit, that was a bit of a guess. Because of that, today I decided to count, and it came to 36 (give or take), so it turns out I did myself a bit of an injustice! It was a fairly standard day in that regard, but the number of photos I was asked for increased dramatically, and I think I was stopped whilst riding at least five times. Ideally, they would ask me when I have already stopped, but I figure people aren't going to be asking for photos or autographs for long, so I may as well be positive about it. I was also stopped by two journalists, which is a first.

India became more rural today, and similar to what I was afraid I would face when coming here. It would have made 100 miles a day pretty difficult had I not had two weeks here already. The smell was not great for a lot of the day either. It seems that the side of the road is often used as a toilet. Not exactly pleasant, but I am surprised I haven't seen more of that. Shows my ignorance I guess.

Anyway, the day was fairly good. I struggled for water at one point, but that was the only problem. Until I reached my finishing point. To cut a long story short, I spent over an hour cycling around Bhimavaram, trying to follow wrong directions and very nearly got my tent out. It destroyed my good mood and has led to less sleep than I was hoping for, although I have calmed down now.

Day 45 – Bhimavaram to Tuni

It was hard getting out of bed this morning. The stress of the evening before meant I didn't get as much sleep as I would've liked. Breakfast consisted of two Snickers, two Mars bars, a decent portion of chocolate cake, some biscuits and a coke. Not exactly savoury, but it gave me a bit of a boost.

Once riding, I felt better. I didn't push the pace, and time passed easily. Having put an extra bottle of water in my bag, I was able to go for longer without stopping, and, despite a quick pause to swap bottles over and to pee, I didn't take much of a break for the first 120 kilometres (about five hours). My contact points (hands, feet and arse) were a bit sore, and glad of the rest when I did eventually stop, but on the whole I still felt fresh.

I'd set out aiming for 105 miles (170 kilometres). However, once I stopped, I realised I would be on for a very early finish; riding at a relaxed pace probably cost me about 20 minutes over those five hours, but riding through the normal 40-kilometre and 80-kilometre food stops saved me over an hour. So, I decided to set my sights on a longer target and got going.

I had a slight cross/tailwind for that last bit of the day, which was brilliant. I was already in a good mindset and that helped too. I can't think of anything interesting or significant that happened I'm afraid, but, until I reached the town I've stopped in, all went really well. Predictably the traffic and signposting was idiotic, but I managed to find a place for the night without too much trouble.

Overall, I'm really pleased with the ride. My body felt great and I would've been fine to do another 10 miles; the next place to stop wasn't for about 15 miles though, and it would have been a stretch to beat sunset. I'm more than happy to leave India without having ridden at night.

Day 46 - Tuni to Srikakulam

Breakfast this morning was, once again, extremely sweet. However, this time it was made up of Indian foods I'd bought the night before, and which I don't know the names of. It was all a bit sickly, and that's something that stayed with me all day. I was craving a massive bowl of cereal today; something along the lines of Chocolate Chip Weetabix Minis, Cheerios, Frosted Shreddies, Special K and Honey Granola by Dorset Cereals, all mixed together in one big bowl! Great endorsement there guys – so if you feel like supplying me with a weekly batch of cereals once I get to university, I'd be more than happy to keep singing your praises.

It turns out that an article has been published about me somewhere in India, which I didn't know about, and I'm not sure where and how. Perhaps due to the enthusiastic hotel owner a couple of days ago? Two guys stopped me for a photo after they had read about my trip. According to them I'm "very awesome"; I'm not ashamed to say that this gave me a much-needed boost! It was also a huge relief, because they had been following me for five minutes and initially I couldn't work out their intentions.

I've just had dinner. After the waiter advised me that what I had ordered was probably too spicy, I went with his recommendation, which, according to him, was not spicy at all. He lied. I think he did it deliberately to see how I'd cope.

100 miles is almost feeling like a short distance now; almost, but not quite ...

Day 47 – Srikakulam to Chatrapur

I didn't organise any breakfast last night, which meant I had no choice but to wait until it was being served downstairs. This meant a late start, so I was a bit stressed right from my alarm, and it became worse as it got harder to fight off the thought that my stomach was not feeling at all good. I'm not sure what it was – I put it down to slight food poisoning – but by the time I was ready to leave, I was struggling not to be sick in the lobby. I've made it 20 days in India without these problems, and it chose to hit me with four days to go. The fact that I am so close to the end is the only reason I got on the bike.

It was not fun: every 10 minutes a wave of nausea would come over me and I am not sure how I kept it down. Time went by agonisingly slowly, so I put my Garmin into my back pocket and just pedalled – doing everything I could to focus on something other than the distance left. Mercifully, the stomach-churning moments became less frequent, and, after about five hours of a seriously unpleasant morning, I started to feel slightly more normal.

My accommodation tonight is on the questionable side, but it has a bed, a toilet and a tap. Unfortunately, the bed has numerous stains on it, the toilet smells better if I don't flush it and the tap is more of a dribble.

Not much else to say about today as I didn't really take much in. If all goes to plan – three days to go, but that might be a significant 'if'.

Additional note: I wrote the above whilst waiting for food. Since walking back to my room

I've stepped in a bag of masala sauce. Initially, I thought it was something else and I was even more displeased!

Day 48 – Chatrapur to Cuttack

Not much happened today. In fact, apart from one idiot asking to buy my bike, nothing of note happened at all.

I felt pretty good all day until about an hour ago. I'm now not feeling good, and I think the only thing to do is to try to get some sleep. Apologies for this everyone. This is not what I wanted so close to the end, and, as long as I can walk, I am going to be riding tomorrow. So, I am just trying to do everything I can now to make tomorrow less unpleasant.

Hopefully, I will be able to share an interesting anecdote tomorrow...

Day 49 – Cuttack to Balasore

This morning was not a fun experience. I woke up numerous times in the night thinking I was about to be sick, so when my alarm went off I wasn't exactly rested. I also wasn't feeling any better, and I could hardly move without feeling ill. It was an hour after I had woken up before I finally managed to get myself together. I still couldn't eat anything, so I set out on an empty stomach.

The only difference to the morning a couple of days ago was the fact that I now had a headwind. The first two hours were the hardest I have had in India, so

I was extremely relieved when I managed to stomach a bit of food at my first stop. Throughout India, eating whilst on the road hasn't offered much variety, and there have been a lot of crisps and biscuits - all of which have been past their sell-by dates. Today was no different, and the crisps I ate were dated last October, which could be the oldest yet.

After the stop, I felt slightly better, but the wind hadn't died down, and I ended up getting a slow puncture. When I first noticed it, I just pumped the tyre back up. This lasted for about 20 minutes before I had to stop again. At this point, I realised there was no use in kidding myself and I may as well change the inner tube. It wasn't so bad - I am more annoyed because it would have been great to be able to say that I only had one puncture in India. I had quite an audience stop to watch me as well, despite being stopped on the side of a dual carriageway!

After fixing it, I inflated the tyres more than normal as I didn't want to take any chances. The ride comfort worsened, but the difference to the speed was also noticeable - and necessary. This delay, along with the headwind, meant that today was a fairly late finish. All my thoughts were of tomorrow, and that helped get me through what was a tough day. I am looking forward to finishing. I think my body may need the rest and I know that my mind does.

At this point, I just want to say a big thanks to all the guys at Condor for their support - especially to Matt, Mindy, Jaz and Angel. The bike is still gorgeous albeit rather dusty...

Day 50 – Balasore to Kolkata

Indian leg done! Over 4,000 kilometres and a fair few curries later, I've cycled both coasts of the country.

This morning started off well. I was in a good mood, and was basically just excited to be so close to the end. I didn't stop much today and probably didn't eat enough, but this last week has had plenty of big days and, despite being ill, my legs handled the distance easily. The ride wasn't without difficulties though, as the first 20 kilometres were dominated by roadworks, and yesterday's headwind had become even stronger. I got frustrated a couple of times, but I cheered up every time I thought of the finish. I can't yet get my head around the fact that a month's worth of cycling is coming to an end. Doing the whole thing without a day off has been worth it, but it has started to have an effect on my body; my arse and hands are going to be very grateful for a couple of days' rest. Finishing and seeing my dad was once again an incredible feeling, but very different from Europe. It's not easy to describe, but today was more like happiness – rather than relief – although there is definitely an element of that as well.

Finishing India remains one of my proudest moments of the whole trip. When I got to the end of that leg, I felt like I had won. I felt genuine joy. Europe had beaten me to my knees; I never felt in control, and by Istanbul I was just thankful to be done. India was the opposite. I had been through my share of difficulties, but I felt like I'd conquered it.

Kolkata highlighted this and made me realise how far I had come in being comfortable with Indian life. When I arrived in

Mumbai, I spent half the time marvelling at everything, and the other half scared out of my mind for what lay ahead. Kolkata was my dad's first visit to India, so I think he must have experienced something similar to my initial feelings, yet, there I was, fazed by very little and no longer interested in the novelty of it all. It was only when I stopped to think about it that I realised how much I had changed.

Moving on to Burma ended my reign of confidence and put me back on level pegging with Dad. In fact, it caused a complete switch. Entering the new and unknown country, I definitely had less composure than he did.

MOTIVATION

I am regularly quizzed on how I stayed motivated. When it got really hard, what made me want to keep pushing? The simple truth – very often there was no motivation. I would frequently wake up and fail to find any positives for getting on the bike that day. On many occasions, riding 100 miles was the last thing that I wanted to do. There's a quote I quite like that I think sums it up really well. It's not overly significant and I don't know who first came up with it – I saw it on a T-shirt someone was wearing in the gym. It read *"Motivation gets you started, attitude keeps you going"*.

Whilst I was struggling over the first few days, weeks and months, Dad would often text me saying, *"It's better than being in school."* He had a point. It's very easy to forget to enjoy something, especially when there's a challenging element involved. Further on in my journey, I would sometimes find myself feeling gloomy, despite experiencing many things that are now cherished memories. Europe was different. I would receive that message and think to myself, *No it fucking isn't.* No part of me wanted to be where I was. I barely even had the will to succeed; I just didn't give myself the option of quitting.

It's not so much a case of cheerfulness in the face of adversity, it's more a case of being seriously miserable and getting on with it regardless. I found it impossible to source fresh motivation every hour of every day, but I think it's the work that is done when there is very little impetus that makes the difference.

I suppose, in reality, I could very easily have stayed in bed and taken a day off whenever I wanted, but if I had attacked the trip with that attitude, I would still be going round. So, even though it generally took multiple alarms and a fair amount of time to get going, I would eventually make it out onto the road, regardless of how I felt about the decision.

Once on the bike, motivation wasn't such an issue. I found it easier not to stop than I did to start off first thing in the morning. Positivity, if you can muster it, does work wonders; no doubt about it. Tell yourself repeatedly that you're feeling good, and you'll start to believe it. It's something I've done on a number of occasions at university, whenever heading out on the bike with a hangover. Sometimes though, it just comes down to gritting your teeth.

The source of any motivation I had, ultimately, came back to the reasons for setting off from London in the first place. I said at the beginning of this book that you would have to wait until the end for those reasons. I can tell you now that the prospect of a potential world record did not come into it. Even if it had been verified by Guinness World Records, it would have served as little more than a nice bonus. Not once did the thought of being the youngest person to cycle around the world ever get me out of bed in the morning.

WHY?
PART 2

Enter Chris:

"I have done a fair bit of motoring around over the last few weeks, and it is quite amazing to see how fashionable cycling has become. I suppose it's nice for families to experience the great outdoors, good to get the kids away from their iPads, good to get the heart pumping, good for old folk with dodgy knees, and great for middle-aged blokes who want to wear Lycra and no longer want to have sex with their long-suffering wives. But I've got no f-ing idea why you're doing it…"

Seeing as you have made it this far, I shall shed a little more light on my reasons for doing something so idiotic. This is not my final answer; that comes later. This is one reason that links in closely with what kept me motivated out on the road.

I love pretty much all sport, so when the Olympics came to London in 2012 I was captivated. I loved seeing the Olympic legends on screen, and I was filled with an enormous amount of motivation and pride in being British. From then on, all I wanted was to make others feel the way I felt towards those athletes. If I could somehow motivate one person to achieve something they otherwise would not, then it would be a job well done. I saw this trip as a way to do that: aspire to inspire.

That was not the sole motivation – riding a bike was already a passion of mine and something I loved doing more than almost anything. To be able to combine this with a way of potentially inspiring others was an opportunity not to be missed.

Once on the road, a lot of my motivation came from thinking of other people back home. I wasn't going to inspire anyone by lying in bed for six months, so I kept moving.

I always get asked why I did this. In the beginning, all I could think to say was, "Why not do this? What possible reason is there to justify not taking on this challenge?" Just because something is difficult is not a reason to turn away; it is the exact opposite.

> *"Nothing in the world is worth having or worth doing unless it means effort, pain, difficulty... I have never in my life envied a human being who led an easy life. I have envied a great many people who led difficult lives and led them well."*
>
> Theodore Roosevelt

FOOD

Whilst riding, I would burn around 5,000 calories a day. I never made a point of tracking this, nor did I wear a heart-rate monitor, so this is a rough estimate rather than an exact number. Irrespective of the actual figure, I knew that I had to eat a lot. Considering I returned the same weight as when I left, I must have succeeded in sourcing enough food. I was in reasonably good shape when I departed, so I didn't have all that much weight to lose. Over the six months, I lost a bit of muscle from my chest and arms, but my legs became a tad bigger to balance it out. It was not something I noticed at the time, but I had to buy new jeans when I returned.

I made a conscious effort to eat anything I could get my hands on, and I couldn't afford to be fussy. The food was mostly good in Europe. It was the kind of food I was used to and what I would consider normal. I ate a lot of pastries, pizza and pasta, but my largest meal came in Tirana (Albania). For dinner, I ordered a main-course-sized portion of lasagne, a large portion of chips, a starter of roasted peppers stuffed with what I assume was feta, and eight chicken fillets (600 grams). When the waiter asked me how much chicken I wanted, I asked what was normal for one person, then tripled it. Admittedly, I was extremely full afterwards, but I left nothing on the plates, and finishing all that felt like an achievement in itself.

The night I was caught in a blizzard in Greece, unlike the hotel I stayed in – which I'm sure was just someone's house – the restaurant I found was genuine. They didn't have a menu though, and instead asked if I wanted pizza or pasta. I ordered both.

Food was generally good throughout Greece; the main reservation I have is that they use far too much onion in their salads. I'm also not the biggest fan of aubergine – and therefore moussaka. I'll eat it, but I'm just not that keen on it. Mind you, I'll eat almost anything that's put in front of me when I'm hungry.

Turkey was great (the country, not the bird), despite only having two or three evenings there. The best meal was a lunch with Dad in Istanbul. We had a range of different meze dishes, which were all great, but I can't actually remember what most of it was. It included a couple of pitas, which are kind of similar to pizzas.

Indian food is world-renowned, and to do it justice requires someone far more knowledgeable than me. Nevertheless, I shall share my thoughts.

As previously mentioned, my memories of India largely depend on how far through the country I was. I value those first couple of weeks extremely highly, but, in a sense, I feel as if I have scratched the itch. Because of this, I am undecided as to whether I would return to the country. I know I'm not ready yet. If I do have a change of heart, one aspect that will lead the way in causing it is the food. It is amazing, and, in my opinion, the number one reason to revisit. Don't get me wrong, I had some truly dreadful meals there (not to mention painful ones), but when you receive a decent one there's nothing else like it.

The good meals I had were almost exclusively in city restaurants. My advice would be to find someone who can take you round, show you the nice places and recommend the best food. Also, be cautious of curries outside of these types of restaurant. If you do have one in a more 'authentic' place, go for the vegetarian option. You can still find tasty meals in rural India; however, they were few and far between during my visit. My preference would be a *biryani*, which obviously comes without sauce. Even in the countryside, they tended to taste a lot better than the alternative dishes. If you want to sample a lot of different things, order a vegetable *thali*.

Make sure you try the various smoothies and juices wherever you are as well. India is famous for them; just be careful with water and ice, of course. Along the same lines, milkshakes/*lassis* are often an essential addition to any meal if you have a Western palate.

Breakfast foods are interesting. The one that I remember is *idli*. It's a rice-based item, so a good thing to eat prior to a long ride. The texture is unlike anything else I have had, but not in a bad way.

Dosas seemed to be the most popular meal I came across. It was recommended by Brits and locals alike. A *dosa* is a crepe-like pancake thing. You can get them plain or with a variety of fillings. My favourite was a *masala dosa*, which comes with a spiced-potato filling.

I also remember the street food tasting good whenever I had it, but look out for how it's stored. Often it is kept out in the warm for hours, which is not ideal if you're hoping to avoid food poisoning. On that note, don't eat fish.

The food in Burma (Myanmar) was a mix between Chinese and traditional Burmese. I enjoyed the Chinese-influenced food. It was surprisingly close to what you would expect to get in Britain, unlike Indian food for which the Western versions are very different to the original. I did not find the traditional Burmese food so appetising, and generally avoided it; I was given a variety of fish pastes on one occasion, which I didn't have fun with, nor the pig's ear I tried in Mandalay.

The Thai food, on this trip, was not as spicy as I expected. I have come to learn that I must have done a good job of sidestepping it. There was a lot of fried rice, which I had few complaints about, and I have previously spoken about how I loved 7-Eleven food throughout the country.

Australia offered food that I was used to, which was mostly good. The only difference was the availability of kangaroo, crocodile and sometimes emu. Kangaroo is really tasty and very lean. Crocodile is also tasty if cooked well.

In the Outback and away from the populated areas, the food was less extravagant, and normally not such good quality. Going through the Nullarbor I survived primarily on chocolate bars. I genuinely started to dislike chocolate because I ate so much of it.

New Zealand was great for food. I had Dad with me then, so I rarely had to think about it. I'd usually meet him at a prearranged distance, and he'd have a selection of things for me to choose from. This often included a pie; it seems they are a mainstay of the Kiwi diet, and they went down surprisingly easily mid-ride.

We went for a couple of good meals when we reached Auckland, and I would thoroughly recommend eating at Elliot Stables. It's a really unique place and has every kind of food you could think of.

Food in the US – for the most part – was shit. As is the case in many countries, it was good until you moved out of the cities. As soon as I did that, I realised how easy it would be to become very fat. Excluding San Francisco, Boston and when I stayed with some friends in New York state, my best meal came in Newport, Oregon. I had been craving a decent cottage pie for a while, and was delighted to find an Irish pub that served one. The only downside was being denied a beer to go with it.

The final leg through Europe was good again. My only night on the road in Portugal was great. I had no idea what I had ordered. The waiter couldn't speak English, so I just pointed to a random item on the menu and hoped for the best. What I got was a perfect post-ride dish. It was an odd mix from a culinary point of view, but I was thrilled. All on the same plate was steak, rice, chips, salad, spinach, some kind of beans, carrots and, what I thought was aubergine. I realised it was, in fact, a grilled banana when I mistakenly tried to eat the skin.

I experienced a huge variety of food throughout my travels, including some amazing meals. Truth be told, I was mostly eating rubbish. During the day, I would eat whatever I could get my hands on, although not once did I go into a McDonald's, Burger King or KFC. They have outlets in every country, but I made a concerted effort not to use them. Despite consciously avoiding these chains, a large portion of my mid-ride meals would still consist of poor-quality carbohydrates and huge amounts of sugar.

NERVES

The nerves first started about a week before I left. Up until that point, the trip hadn't felt real. Although the planning and the training had been going on for months, departure always seemed like a long way off. With a week to go, I suddenly realised how close it was. Over that week the stress built up and up, until the final night where I collapsed into bed having spent the evening panicking about last-minute details.

On the morning of my departure, I was oddly relaxed. I wasn't nervous and I wasn't even excited; my head was empty. I felt detached from the whole thing. I couldn't quite believe that it was actually happening. Whatever I was feeling when I made my first pedal strokes, it wasn't nerves.

The situation was different that night on the ferry to France. After an emotional goodbye with my family, I was left alone with my thoughts. The nerves definitely returned then. I had absolutely no clue what I was doing, how I would do it or what to expect. The concept of 18,000 miles seemed like such an impossible distance. Even now, I can't get my head around it. All I could think about on that crossing was that I had perhaps made a very big mistake in being so ambitious.

As the trip went on, I became more comfortable with what I was doing. That does not mean that I stopped feeling nervous, which generally stemmed from a fear of the unknown. Whenever I was unsure how the next week, day or hour would pan out, or when confronted with something new, I would get some form of nerves; for example, when it first started snowing on me, my first night in a tent or when riding into a new country. The last of those was the most frequent, and when I felt the most on edge. I liked settling into a routine. It made it easy to break the days down, and it meant I didn't have to worry as much about things. I would get used to shopping in the same kind of shops, eating the same foods and even riding for the same distances between breaks. Crossing an international border threw all this up in the air.

Whilst some border crossings presented only subtle changes, there were others that were far more drastic. Flying from Europe to India didn't just challenge my cycling routine, it flipped every single thing I knew about life on its head. During my two days in Mumbai, the nerves were ever present. Those days were essential and enjoyable, but making no tangible progress to my mileage only exacerbated my anxiety.

Burma was even worse. This surprised me at the time, considering I had just spent a month riding through India. After finishing that leg, I hadn't thought I would be fazed at all, but when I arrived in Mandalay I was bricking it. On the surface, it was nowhere near as intimidating as India, but, as I started to think about the coming days, I realised I knew absolutely nothing about anything. As an example, the maps on my Garmin didn't have any roads in the right place, and other online maps were largely inaccurate as well. Furthermore, as a tourist, according to Burmese laws I could only stay in specific registered hotels. Mum had tried to contact the embassy there,

Two days before departure. Very naive and still undecided about the contents of my panniers.

About to set off and eager to get going (despite what my face suggests). Photo credit: Meryl Herniman.

Prior to paying a fortune for Turkish Delight in the Istanbul spice bazaar.

Even with 10 elephants and a festival in the middle of the road, the locals still stared at me.

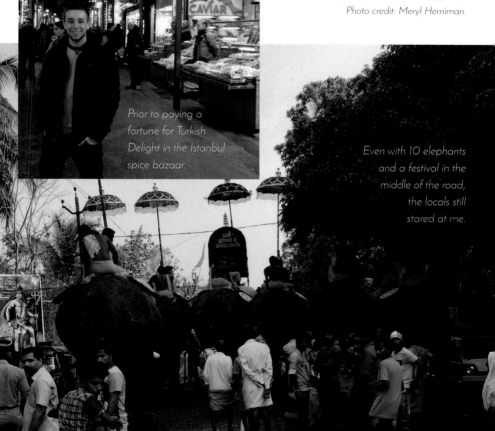

These guys cheered me up. Can't say I've ever been that happy to see a picture of my own face.

Yes, I'm wearing flowers!

End of the India leg, it all felt a bit surreal.

Outside the bike shop (shack) in Kolkata.

I wasn't miserable the whole time. This climb in Burma put me in a good mood... until I nearly slipped off the edge of the cliff 10 minutes later.

If I'd ridden a little bit faster, I could have been under that.

Riding through a 'controlled' forest fire in Australia was not a highlight. Smoke and exercise don't mix.

One of the many long, straight roads. The smile was probably forced.

90 MILE STRAIGHT
AUSTRALIA'S LONGEST STRAIGHT ROAD
146.6 km

The Great Ocean Road.

That was a fun day...

*London Arch (formerly London Bridge)
off the Great Ocean Road.*

*Everyone at Abbotsleigh School
gave me a fantastic farewell
as I left Sydney.*

Starting the New Zealand leg from Dunedin in the early hours of the morning. Felt weird (in a very good way) having my dad with me.

Signs like this one really cheered me up.

After descending from snow-capped mountains in Washington state, I found myself riding into what appeared to be another desert.

Tan lines in their prime. I turned
many heads at that beach.

Reaching the end of mainland Europe
and trying to keep a lid on my emotions.

A well-earned beer with Nige and Henry on the ferry crossing back to the UK.
Capping off an awesome final week with them and Dad.

I managed to hold back the tears for all of 30 seconds.

Job done.
Photo credit: Paul Kenward.

No words.
Photo credit: Angela Newman.

but it was impossible to get through by telephone, fax or email. In fact, six months after I returned to London, she received an email from one of the embassy staff in Burma apologising for being behind on picking up emails!

All this meant I couldn't just arrive in a town and try to find a room. Essentially, I had to plan – or at least have an idea of – where I would be staying each night. With this lack of flexibility, the stress increased hugely. On top of this, there were the usual jitters about finding food on the road and not being able to speak the language.

Thankfully, when I arrived in Mandalay I was put in touch with a native English speaker, and she addressed a lot of my worries. She gave me a map of the country, and circled places along my route where she thought I would be able to stay. I calmed down a bit after that meeting, and was then able to concentrate on sorting my bike out.

For reasons I will soon explain, I was right to be nervous about Burma. However, being able to settle a few concerns before I set off left me feeling a lot more confident.

Arriving in Burma proved to be the most difficult change of country for me, but even later in my journey, when I was crossing into Canada from the US, I remained apprehensive about a number of aspects. I still panicked about what to expect, despite everything being relatively similar.

Portugal and Spain were different again. (My final countries of France and England posed no problem as I knew them well and had company with me.) After dropping my focus when I reached Boston, the day before departure in Lisbon, I felt sick all day. Rushing to try to get everything sorted, I maintained very little composure. It took me about a week to get my head properly back in the game, and, throughout Spain, I still found myself worrying constantly.

Nerves were inevitable in something like this. Arguably, they are a good thing too; complacency was the enemy in a lot of instances. The thing I found odd was that nerves would often find me at unexpected points, and yet were absent at the obvious occasions, such as Day 1 or starting across the Nullarbor Plain in Australia. When planning the trip, the Outback was one of the most daunting prospects, however, I was just happy to have reached that point, rather than nervous, when I eventually got there.

HEAT

Surprisingly, high temperatures had more of an overall impact than low ones. Sure, when the temperature dropped significantly it made me miserable, it made everything unpleasant and I would still prefer searing deserts over icy winds. Despite that, it turned out to be the heat that came closer to breaking me physically.

India was the first time I encountered any form of warmth. I had spent the previous three weeks acclimatising to the sub-zero temperatures of Europe. My body then had to deal with a temperature swing of close to 50°C. It's quite interesting how great an effect the temperature can have on performance. Whilst your body will adjust over time and become more used to whatever climate you train in, if you take yourself straight from one extreme to the other, you are going to struggle.

My first few days in India were not straightforward, and I often ended up in a salty mess slumped on the side of the road, with my head spinning out of control. Imagine doing 10 shots of vodka in a sauna and you might feel something similar.

The main issues came on the hills. Not only did my effort increase, but my speed dropped and the air flow cooling me down became non-existent. It was humid as well, which only added to the amount of fluid I was losing.

Since being at Loughborough University, I have participated in a PhD student's research study, part of which entailed looking at cycling performance in the heat. In short, I was put on a bike in a 30°C chamber without a fan, and asked to pedal really hard. It transpired that my power dropped over 15% from my normal performance. That's a significant difference, and it took place in a controlled environment whilst maintaining hydration. When I then looked back at the hotter moments of my trip, it was nice to know that my suffering was unavoidable and completely normal.

As I moved through India, I became better at dealing with the scorching temperatures. In part, this was due to there being fewer hills after the first week. More than that though, my body started to acclimatise, and I was able to gauge more accurately how close I was to overheating. It never actually got too bad (relatively speaking). The worst occasion in India was on the second or third day. It took me about an hour to recover after cresting a climb, and, whilst I was very dehydrated, I felt nothing more than physically drained and a bit dizzy – nothing too serious. Burma was a different story all together, and something I'll explain shortly.

Unexpectedly, I encountered my maximum temperature (46°C) in the US. When planning my route, I decided to ride through the northern states to avoid the heat of Texas and Arizona in summer. Unfortunately, those northern states experienced a heatwave that surpassed anything they've had in the last 15 years or so.

That heat didn't come with the humidity of Asia, but it still presented a considerable challenge. I learnt that 40°C was my body's cut-off. I had become fairly good at handling temperatures up to that point, but as soon as it hit +40°C, my heart rate would rocket upwards, and I would start guzzling water by the litre. This caught me off guard one day in Montana. I misjudged the distance between shops (it ended up being 30 miles), and, although I had refilled my water, I hadn't catered for the hill that was to come, nor the fact that the sun remained directly above me for the entire stretch.

I avoided any significant problems, but, when I stopped at the next petrol station, I did need to stand in the frozen food aisle for a good 10 minutes to cool down. A litre of Powerade also went a long way to helping me recover, and, on this occasion, I was grateful for the US' extreme portion sizes. I was verging on severe dehydration at that point, but, compared to what I faced in Burma, it was nothing.

I wasn't worried about the heat when I landed in Mandalay. I assumed I had faced everything already in India and that it wouldn't pose any issues. I was wrong. The temperature averaged only 3°C or 4°C warmer, but that made all the difference. Day 53 (Day 3 in Burma) was horrendous and amongst the worst three of the whole trip (to go with the knee issues on Day 6, and Day 14 in Croatia).

The day topped out at 44°C, but, on top of this, I had a (warm) headwind. It felt like I was riding into a hairdryer, and meant I was working twice as hard without realising. I had a choice that day: I could stop at either 100 kilometres or 160 kilometres. Due to the hotel restrictions, there was no other alternative. Stopping at the earlier one would have a knock-on effect on the following days, so I aimed for the longer option. This was a mistake. I was already struggling when I reached the town at 100 kilometres. I sat on the pavement for close to 80 minutes, trying to get my body back into working order. It took me two minutes to open a bottle of water because my forearm kept cramping up. I was already feeling dizzy, and, in hindsight, I definitely should have stopped there. However, I had already set my mind on the further option, and, being a stubborn bastard, I wasn't about to give up.

I'm still not sure how I let myself get so bad. I didn't drink or eat any less than normal; something just stopped working. With the wind in my face, I was averaging 20 km/h, which meant I had another three hours' riding to go after realising my body was against the ropes. I don't remember everything from the last part of that day, but it felt like my body was shutting down.

I started getting cramp in places I didn't even know I had muscles. I was struggling to keep my eyes open, and, whenever I yawned, my whole jaw and tongue would go into spasm. By the time I reached the final hour, I was having to stop every 10 minutes for just as long to recover.

By this point, I didn't know what was going on around me, but, with 10 kilometres to go, I pulled into a petrol station and collapsed onto a bench, utterly depleted. One of the people working there brought me some water, although they even had to open the bottle for me when they realised I couldn't do it. Three litres later, some of which was poured over my head, I felt a bit better. My muscles still weren't responding, but I was able to focus on what I was doing. I owe a huge thank you to those people who took care of me. I tried to pay when I was leaving, but they wouldn't accept any money.

Looking back now, I find it quite worrying. I was in a really bad way, and probably wasn't far off doing some serious damage to myself. Those locals saved me from this and didn't ask for anything in return. I had turned up out of the blue, unable to speak their language, yet they took it upon themselves to help me. I find it odd to think that they had such a large impact on me, despite the fact I wouldn't even know what they looked like if I ever saw them again. Strange really, but when you move away from 'developed countries', you realise that people can be, and often are, 'very awesome'.

The final 10 kilometres were still excruciating. To make matters worse, I ended up riding an additional 10 kilometres after that due to a communication error regarding my accommodation. For the same reason, I ended up staying in an unlicensed hotel, which was what I had been trying to avoid in the first place, and the whole reason for the day's mishaps.

This was one of the few occasions I played down the day's events when I wrote my blog. I think part of me was too exhausted at the time to go on about it, but I was also wary of people worrying about me. It's funny, but there were a number of times where I felt other people's stress, even though that stress was because of what I was going through.

The evening was just as crap. The place I was staying was an absolute toilet, and dinner was far from the recovery meal I needed. I barely slept that night either. I kept waking up in a state of delirium thinking I had to rush off. I eventually gave into those urges and got out of bed at 5am.

I was alive (obviously), but my body was working harder than I ever thought possible. I set out on this trip to see if I could find my breaking point. I wanted to prove to myself that I could push my mind further than my body. I think I very nearly succeeded. On that day, had I been required to carry on, I think I would have been mentally capable of running my body completely into the ground. I don't necessarily think that's a good thing. Once I'd come to my senses, it took me a good few days to get over the shock of it all. I surprised myself with how deep I went, and, although it's something I'm now proud of, I am yet to decide if it's a positive.

BURMA

I loved Burma. I know it is now called Myanmar, but the British Government still referred to it as Burma when I went, so that's what I got used to and what I'm going to continue using. As a side note, Myanmar is pronounced *Me-an-mar*, not *My-an-mar* as I had assumed before getting there. Heat exhaustion on my third day somewhat limited my fondness for the country, but, in hindsight, it was definitely one of my favourites, and a place I would recommend venturing to – leaving aside the recent political troubles.

I arrived in Mandalay – the former capital city – after spending three weeks in the chaos of India. I had no idea what to expect when I arrived, and I was pleasantly surprised. This is a paragraph from my blog after my first day of riding there:

When I say Burma is similar to India, it's not really. But, in terms of cycling across it, my routine is similar (at least, it was today). The drivers aren't great, but they're a lot better than in India, and there are also far fewer of them. The people are still extremely friendly, but they don't force themselves on you.

They're all largely satisfied with a "hello" rather than a full interview – so that's quite nice. The tap water remains undrinkable, but the locals all drink bottled water anyway, so there's much less of an issue when trying to get it. My food whilst cycling still comes from roadside stalls, and it's still bloody hot. Basically, from my point of view, it's like a cleaner, quieter India. And it's been really good so far.

I would consider both India and Burma to be developing countries. However, in this endeavour, I believe India is a bit screwed. I don't want to offend anyone with the following sentiment, so please humour me.

For the whole of India to reach a point of development akin to Western Europe or somewhere similar, someone needs to hit a reset button. I'm not saying that it needs to aspire towards this; I think India is unique, and I believe it would be a tragedy if the country in its current form were to vanish. The thing is, the cars, the traffic and the way the cities are built prevents much more expansion. For traffic to work like it does in London, every car would have to be scrapped, the roads would have to be rebuilt and everyone would have to retake their driving test – legitimately this time. This principle applies to a lot of things; the wealth differential is so vast in India that without flattening people's homes or even entire cities, further expansion is going to be difficult. At the very least, it is going to be extremely slow.

I did not see that problem with Burma. It still has bad drivers and it still doesn't have drinkable tap water, but that's the same with Thailand. With Burma, there's room for expansion and there is still space on the roads for cars to move around. I appreciate I'm focusing a lot on the state of the traffic, but I think that's the one thing in India that will be hardest to change. I may be naive in saying all this, but I'm just trying to describe how I felt Burma differed from India. It is essentially a mix of India and Thailand. It's India, but with a sense of order. I'm ignoring the political issues that are still present in Burma. Thankfully, I saw very little evidence of any problems and do not know enough about them to comment.

When I set off from Mandalay, I was feeling a mixture of emotions. I was scared, I was eager to get going and I was dreading leaving Dad. I cried every time I left my family. Whether it was in Istanbul airport, Singapore or Auckland, I would always ride or walk away, and start crying. I can't properly describe the feeling. It wasn't only the sadness of leaving them – perhaps it was fear of what was ahead, I'm not sure – but it happened every time, no matter how hard I tried to avoid it or how short I kept the goodbyes.

The relative calm of Burma helped. It allowed me to relax and settle into riding my bike quicker than normal. I still wasn't overly cheerful on the first morning, until I was flagged down by an English guy who had stopped his car just ahead of me. He told me he was late for work so couldn't stop to talk, but he gave me a packet of biscuits and a drink, then drove off again.

From that moment, my mood got exponentially better. The locals were all so friendly, and every single one greeted me with a smile. When I got to my hotel room at the end of the day, I looked in the mirror and burst out laughing. I had been particularly nervous about Burma and how I was going to manage, and all my nerves eased in that moment.

The next day finished a bit differently. I had planned my stop for the new capital city – Naypytaw. I spent what felt like hours riding the last 20 kilometres through the outskirts of the city. It was one of the weirdest places I have been.

It has been purpose built to cater for huge expansion; the trouble is, there is very little going on there at the moment. Consequently, I found myself riding on a 16-lane highway that was completely empty. If you have seen the Top Gear episode where they go to Burma with trucks, at one point they play football in the middle of a very wide road – that's where I was. It wasn't quite empty enough that I could start a football game, but I could happily ride in the middle lane without any worries.

Once the novelty wore off, I realised I had absolutely no clue where I was, nor how far I was from a hotel. Maps of the new Burmese roads were hard to come by, my Garmin was useless, and my phone didn't have a signal. The wide road also skewed my perception of distance, and, when paired with the heat, I started to feel rather lost.

I'm assuming there is a city centre in Naypytaw, but despite riding for a good 40 minutes, I never saw it. I never even saw any buildings apart from regularly spaced police huts. I knew that all the hotels were in a specific *hotel district*, and I knew that this district was near a golf course. So, with a rapidly emptying water supply, and without any way of reading the road signs, I stopped to ask the policemen in the little huts for directions. Unfortunately, none of them spoke English, so I had to resort to miming. I did this a lot in India when trying to find places to stay. I would act out going to sleep and people tended to catch on pretty quickly. For some reason, this did not work in Burma; perhaps they sleep in funny positions. Anyway, I decided instead to act out a golf swing in the hope that they'd point me towards the golf course. I'm not sure whether they knew what I was asking or whether they were just trying to get rid of me, but, after stopping and asking three times, I eventually found myself on a slightly smaller boulevard. This one only had six lanes on each side, but it was lined with lots of very big hotels. All of which seemed to be open and all of which seemed to be empty.

I rode along, attempting to find a cheaper one, but they were all huge, resort-type places. The road and hotels were so big that I couldn't see how far the district went on for. So, after riding past at least 10 hotels, I gave up and pulled into one that looked slightly less glamorous than the others. As it happened, the hotels continued for five kilometres, so I needn't have worried.

The following day was Day 53, when I suffered what must have a been a severe case of heat exhaustion. I have already had a good moan about that, so I'll move on. Day 4 in Burma was shorter, and I went about it cautiously. I was in shock from the state I had got myself into the previous day.

I started riding at 6.30am having had a torrid night's sleep. I woke almost every 40 minutes, either cramping or in a weird state of confusion. I had very few options regarding where I could stay that night, so I only had a 70-mile day ahead of me; something I was very grateful for.

I spent the day in damage control. My body was still suffering from the previous day's efforts, and my mind was very wary of the problems I would encounter if I went over that edge again. I stopped regularly and before I needed to. The day passed without incident. It was a game of patience, and resulted in five hours of riding conservatively and fighting off boredom.

Starting off the next day, the ride ahead of me was a bit of an unknown quantity. I knew I would have to stop in Hpa-An, which was 125 miles away, because, from there, it was a full day's ride until the next place I could stop at, just over the Thai border. The question was whether to ride to Hpa-An in one day, or stop for the night at 55 miles and spread the 125 miles over two days.

Naturally, there were a few additional logistical problems to navigate, so it wasn't a straightforward decision and it wasn't based purely on how my legs felt. Had that been the case, I would have pushed for the longer option. However, if I did that, it would put me a day ahead of schedule for when I had planned to meet my family, just south of Bangkok. This would mean I had a day of doing nothing before my parents arrived – which seemed pointless – and I would then struggle to get through the rest of Thailand afterwards on my 15-day visa.

As it happened, I would be given a 30-day visa when I entered Thailand, but I didn't know that at the time. I went back and forth between my options continually for the first couple of hours of the ride:

After much deliberation, I decided on the short day. I wasn't exactly sure how close I was going to be on the 15-day deadline, so it was more of a 'play it safe' decision.

Ten minutes later, I looked at the time and changed my mind. My legs felt good, and could have gone the whole 55 miles without a break, which would have put me at an 11am finish. I decided it was a cop-out to stop that early, and therefore focused on the longer target.

Another 10 minutes went by, and I changed my mind again. I couldn't get the visa problem out of my head, and I pulled up for something to eat. I stopped long enough to put the option of a windy 200-kilometre day out of the question. So, from there, my finish was set.

I wasn't totally happy with my decision, but it was definitely the right one. It turns out that I can't afford to have an extra day in Thailand. Regardless, I was a bit frustrated with myself and decided that, once at the hotel, I would ditch my panniers and go for a quick ride somewhere. Thankfully, I relaxed a bit, realised this was a stupid idea, and instead settled for pushing hard into the headwind that had somehow decided to stick around.

I'm now staying just outside of the town [Kyaikto], and, after deciding to venture in for a look, I discovered why I see so few people doing anything in the sun. By the time I'd finished a half-hour walk and got back to my room, I was drenched. It's not like I didn't already stick out either. I'm probably the only white guy in the area, I was the only person out walking in the sun and, to add to that, I was absolutely dripping in sweat... I drew quite a few looks. Fortunately, I've grown used to that.

Apart from my introduction to 'what not to do in Burma', I spent most of my long afternoon at the restaurant ordering from the pork menu or chicken menu. Each had exactly the same dishes on offer, the only difference being the meat. I sampled a fair bit of it, and can conclude that tonight, chicken ended on top. I think I had about eight or nine courses between 3pm and 7pm.

All that remained of Burma after that was two days' riding and an evening in Hpa-An; another of the few places in Asia, where I didn't feel out of place. One of the main reasons for it being such a tourist hub is some large caves, but I didn't go to see them as they were a little way out of the town.

As for the riding, until I reached a very suspect road in the latter part of the second day (something I will elaborate on in the next chapter), both days passed with only a couple of notable moments.

The first of these was when I came uncomfortably close to getting taken out by a concrete pillar. A truck driver forgot to put his handbrake on, and his vehicle rolled down a hill before crashing into a telegraph pole. It caused a big electric spark, and the whole thing fell in the road about 20 metres in front of me.

The second break from the monotony was an unusual encounter with an unusual woman. She was driving her scooter along next to me and chatting away in a language I didn't understand. After a short while, she gestured for me to pull over and then tried to convince me to put my bike on the back of her scooter – something that would never have worked. I think she was offering me a lift, but, for all I know, she could have been asking to take my bike for good. Whichever it was, I declined with a smile.

She then stopped me again 200 metres further along the road, this time by slamming on the brakes in front of me. She handed me a laminated A4 picture of two women (one of whom I think was her), and drove off again. I don't know why she did that, but I suppose it was a nice gesture. It was strange, but not quite as forward as the woman in Thailand a few days later who asked me to marry her daughter. True story. I can't remember how I talked my way out of that one.

Burma was all a bit of a blur. I had a vast range of experiences there, and I now have very positive feelings towards the country. Not something I can say for many places. I genuinely think the people were the friendliest I happened upon.

CLIMBS

Riding uphill is a brilliant remedy for almost any problem. A long climb can offer an escape for people of all dispositions, whether you are after a platform to really test yourself or you just want to revel in stunning mountain views. For me, riding up a mountain is a physical challenge in its purest form. It allows me to clear my head of everything save for the pain in my legs and the pain in my lungs. Even if that's not your thing, once it's over you'll surely take pleasure in the feeling of conquering whatever mountain you find yourself on.

I have been very fortunate in that I've been able to spend time riding my bike in the French Alps. It offers challenges and scenery that you'll be hard pressed to find anywhere else. When I first thought about taking my bike to different destinations around the globe, searching for magnificent climbs in exotic countries was a large part of the plan.

When my idea developed to include more miles and a much heavier bike, climbs became something I actively avoided. Nevertheless, I shall briefly describe a few of the more notable ones I came across.

Dad was the one planning the specifics of my route, so he

was in charge of finding ways around the big hills. Considering I rode 18,000 miles and I only have a handful to talk about, he did a very good job. Obviously, I won't mention every climb I did, as that would get rather boring. I am also going to ignore all the climbs I actively disliked, which includes all those I did during the five days riding over the Great Dividing Range in Australia. I was tired, the roads were busy, and my knee hurt.

LE TESTANIER (JUST OUTSIDE FRÉJUS, FRANCE)
5.2 KILOMETRES, 5% AV. GRADIENT

The Côte d'Azur is renowned for its cycling prestige. Pro cyclists flock to Cannes, Nice and Monaco to set up base there. The climate is kind most of the year, the scenery is stunning and there are hills aplenty.

This climb came on the morning of Day 9, when I was still in desperate need of a pick-me-up. The sun was out, and it was absolutely sublime. I had never ridden around there before, and this served as the perfect introduction. It gave me a brief sample of what the area has to offer, and left me itching to go back.

There are many others in the area – which I'm sure are just as good, if not better – but I would still say this one is worth seeking out if you are close by. I had Dad with me (and carrying a couple of my panniers), which made things significantly easier and more enjoyable. After the tough first week I'd had, this climb served as a release for a lot of the stress I had built up. Descending the other side, I had a constant smile on my face. It was also the first time I encountered any other cyclists on my trip, and I took great pleasure in mixing in amongst them, despite my still partially laden bike. One to remember.

CLIMB OUT OF SENJ (CROATIA)
8.7 KILOMETRES, 4% AV. GRADIENT

Another instance of morning therapy. This climb, on Day 15, came immediately after what remains the most miserable evening I have ever had on a bike. I had been riding through snow the night before, but, on this morning, the sun was out, and, although still only 2°C, I worked up enough of a sweat to feel comfortable taking my gloves off. The views over the Adriatic Sea were breathtaking. The whole coastline must be a magnificent place to visit in the summer months.

CLIMB LEADING TO MYAWADDY
(BURMA-THAILAND BORDER)
16.4 KILOMETRES, 4% AV. GRADIENT

To provide some context – this is more about the road than the climb. The road is one of the main routes to the Thai border, and, aside from some vague warnings, I knew very little about what was ahead of me. I had heard that, due to the condition of the road, they alternate the traffic direction each day, although I was not certain about that. However, if that was the case, I had no way of knowing which way the traffic would be going when I got there. I have only read about one other cyclist who took this route, and he got on a bus for this section. At the time of writing this, only four people (including me) have covered the climb on Strava. So, in summary, it is not a popular cycling route.

This is from my blog:

Upon arriving at the base of the climb, I found a queue of about five cars, and a barrier across the road. At the time, it looked as if they alternated traffic every few hours, so I carried on without stopping. It would take me a long time to get over the climb anyway, so I figured there was no point waiting. Once going uphill, I felt great. The road was a bit crap and it was narrow, but I was the only one on it, and I was loving it.

I spent the first 30 minutes expecting a big wave of trucks to come down in the opposite direction. Instead, the opposite happened, and I caught the back of an extremely long and very stationary-looking queue. Skipping the line generally wasn't too much of an issue, although, being uphill and largely through gravel, it had its difficulties. At one point, I came close to slipping off a steep drop whilst going round a truck, but other than that the only issue was the slow progress. After a while, I reached the front end of the line, and discovered the source of the hold up. Basically, any time a truck reached a hairpin bend (there were a lot of trucks and a lot of hairpins) it took minutes for it to get round. How this has ended up as the only route to one of the main border crossings is beyond me.

Once in front of the slower-moving vehicles, I had the road to myself again (the surface had got worse though). Every so often, a truck would come past, followed by a few cars, but then there would be another big gap until the next lot. Having seen the road and the traffic, it makes sense that they alternate the traffic daily; so I guess it was lucky that I caught it on the right day. Having said that, I probably would've gone up regardless, which could have led to a few stains in my cycling shorts.

I am still none the wiser as to how that road is meant to operate. I made it through just about alive, so I didn't bother to query it. I am hoping that there is now a new road in place to provide a safer route to the border. If there isn't, it really should be on their to-do list.

The whole thing was an exhilarating experience. I spent a lot of it with the smell of burning clutch in my nose, but having your back wheel slide off the edge of a cliff offers a unique adrenaline rush. It was incredible. Even without the novelty, the views on offer were superb. My tip to anyone thinking of attempting the climb (not something I can recommend with a clear conscience) is to stick to the inside of the road whenever possible, but beware of falling rocks.

TWO CLIMBS OUT OF MAE SOT (THAILAND)

The very next day started with two of the more challenging ascents of the trip. The first was about eight kilometres long and mostly about 8–10% average gradient, excluding a couple of short, flat sections. The second climb was 12 kilometres long at the same gradient, although, in addition to this, it had sections that kicked up to 14%. With the weight I was carrying, doing the two climbs back to back presented an arduous morning.

On the first climb, I was able to let myself be distracted by the countless people farming locusts. There must have been many millions of the insects on that climb. It was cool to see, but even more amazing to hear. I have never heard living creatures create such a loud and consistent noise. I could barely even hear myself when I started encouraging my legs onwards. I stopped at the top, but not for very long. The din was hurting my ears.

By the time I started the second ascent, I was having to work hard. I was no longer able to pay much attention to the wildlife, and was instead focused solely on keeping the bike moving. Cresting the second climb was a great feeling. After dropping down the other side, I would have 1,000 miles of pan-flat riding until the Malaysian rainforest. I was therefore able to fully appreciate the descent, on what was a perfect road surface:

> Going down the other side was fantastic, and I couldn't help a grin spreading across my face. My euphoria was somewhat interrupted by two passing cars though. (In my defence, it was a slightly flatter section.) Just after overtaking me, the rear window of the first car rolled down. A chubby kid poked his head out and was sick everywhere. I'll admit I was a bit shocked at first, but after checking that my bike and I were vomit-free, I took great pleasure in seeing that the following car wasn't. I laughed the rest of the way down.

HIGHWAY 1, BETWEEN ROCKPORT AND SOUTH LEGGETT (CALIFORNIA, US)
11.2 KILOMETRES, MOSTLY 6%, SOME FLAT, AND THE LAST KILOMETRE AT 10% GRADIENT

My second day in California produced the most climbing of any single day in my whole trip, and it finished with this climb. After a day of riding along a picturesque and rolling coastline, I turned my back to the sea and headed into the bigger hills. It was nothing too challenging, but it was steep enough to hurt and long enough to forget a frustrating day. I put a lot more effort than was necessary into this one, and I almost felt as though I was riding a lightweight bike.

The road was quiet, the surface smooth and the scenery a sight for sore eyes. Not mountain views of the coastline, but thick redwood forest. They weren't quite the giant redwoods I would encounter the following day, but were essentially the baby equivalents.

WHITE PASS (WASHINGTON, US)
24.8 KILOMETRES, 4% AV. GRADIENT

On Day 129, I stopped heading north through the western states and turned east. This meant dealing with the Rockies. Due to my dad's superb route planning, I got the majority of the mountain range out of the way with only one climb, having expected to cycle over huge passes for consecutive days.

White Pass itself is a gorgeous climb. From memory, the gradient never goes over 8%, so it's easy to get into a rhythm. The views are stunning whenever the forest thins out, and I even glimpsed the snow line not too far off.

The best part though, was the descent down the other side. It had perfectly smooth tarmac; wide, sweeping bends; and views to challenge the Alps. I finished the day on a plateau two-thirds of the way down, with another huge smile on my face.

Nothing I ascended on this trip challenged the extreme ends of the Alps or the Pyrenees, and, riding such a heavy bike, I was relieved about that. Any short rise felt significant, and these climbs were more than adequate in providing a challenge. As I said, these are by no means the only climbs I rode up during my journey, but they are the few I would have regretted missing.

TAN LINES

Along with hairless legs, outrageous tan lines are an easy way to identify a cyclist. The two go hand in hand: the smoother the legs, the easier they tan.

I took great pride in my tan lines during my travels, and whenever it was sunny I made a point of ensuring my shorts were at exactly the same level as the previous day, for maximum sharpness. Obsessive, I know, and many of you may think less of me for doing something so ridiculous, but, let's face it, I didn't always have a lot to keep me entertained.

The truth is, they served as a badge of honour for me. Unlike in some other sports, cyclists don't develop big muscles that they can show off – they develop tan lines. Mine were a result of over 1,200 hours in the saddle and proof of my long days in the sun. I often get people questioning the legitimacy of my trip and asking how they can know I didn't just catch a bus. I realise that this is generally said in jest, but one needed only to look at my multi-coloured skin to see I was telling the truth. If that's not enough for you, I carried a tracker the whole time and uploaded all of my rides to the internet. So, had I taken a bus, it would have been moving very slowly.

The first month through Europe provided very little in the way of sun, and not a single day of temperatures warm enough to brandish my thighs. India was the first opportunity, and, whilst the weather provided a good base, the baggy shorts I wore over my Lycra prevented anything overly spectacular coming to fruition.

Southeast Asia was when I began to stand out, and it wasn't just my legs and arms. My ankle tan lines ensured I looked positively ridiculous in flip flops. However, it was my gloves that produced arguably my strangest tan lines. Being fingerless, my hands remained pale, but my fingers were tanned, and it looked as though I had been involved in something extremely unsavoury.

To my dismay, my tan lines faded over the two months I spent in the southern hemisphere. Autumn and winter in Australia and New Zealand provided scarce amounts of precious UV radiation.

Whilst I was not overly pleased to be greeted by a heatwave in the US, it did offer one saving grace in that my legs were able to return to their former prime.

The final 12 days from Lisbon up through Europe offered a last dose of sun, which would secure my status as a first-rate zebra. At the end of Day 168 in Mimizan (on the west coast of France), I made a brief trip to the beach with Dad and Henry. It had been a while since I had done something so normal, and I felt extremely out of place. Over the months leading up to that, I learnt to stop caring about pretty much everything, but I suddenly became very aware of the number of heads that followed me as I walked by. I got used to it in India, but in a country where staring would usually be frowned upon, I felt a bit self-conscious.

A few days later, on the ferry crossing from France back to England, having near enough circumnavigated the globe, a woman literally pointed and laughed at my sock tan lines. I was a bit taken aback. I was heading back to my seat, after a well-earned beer on the deck with Dad, Henry and Nige, when this far-from-discreet woman felt the need to alert the rest of the ship to my abnormalities. Once over my initial shock though, I was able relax in the knowledge that my tan lines really were a sight to behold, and a task successfully completed. I strolled the rest of the way back to my seat, smugly allowing people to bask in the glow emanating from my outrageously orange legs.

A month and a half later, I started my first term at university, tan lines still sharp. I remained far too proud of them. However, by this point, I had come to realise that I did, in fact, look like a total fucking idiot.

BORDER CROSSINGS

I had 16 borders to negotiate on my travels. Whilst most of those in the EU offered nothing more than a sign to let me know I was changing country, there were some further afield that required a little more effort on my part.

Most border guards would take an interest in my trip. Perhaps I was a novelty when compared to the hundreds of cars they saw go past every day, especially when they noticed the stamps I had collected in my passport.

The crossing into Montenegro from Croatia presented more than the regular conversation though. As I approached the border, I had not realised that there were two checkpoints to pass through. I now understand this is common practice. There was one for leaving Croatia and another one for entering Montenegro. However, in this case, there was over a kilometre between the two, which confused me. I showed my passport as normal at the first checkpoint, and was waved through without trouble. Upon arriving at the second, I was in the queue behind a car, when the man in the little booth gestured for me to go to the adjacent lane, which looked shut. I managed to misinterpret these random arm movements as, "Go straight through, you're okay." It turns out I was wrong, and was promptly shouted at. I returned to the office where I was met by a stern woman, who looked as though she would have jumped at any opportunity to send me all the way back to England. Thankfully, after an awkward minute or two, I was allowed through without any real harm done.

Burma to Thailand was a whole different ball game, and a unique experience for me. First and foremost, it is the only time in my life that I have stood in a crowd and felt tall. It was wonderful.

Leaving Burma only took a few minutes. The authorities weren't prepared for cyclists, and seemed unsure as to whether I should be treated as a car or a pedestrian. So, after briefly taking me into an office and checking I was not a criminal, they allowed me through. The bridge between the two checkpoints was interesting in itself because they drive on a different side of the road in Burma to Thailand. I'm not sure what they do in other places where this happens, but, in this case, there was no clever system for swapping lanes, there was just a sign to tell you to do so halfway along the bridge.

After crossing to the left-hand lane, I reached the Thai side of the border. There, I was presented with a few difficulties. There were *a lot* of very loud and probably confused people, and it was 15 minutes before I found anyone in a position of authority who had some basic English. I had actually passed through the barriers by this point, and, as I approached him, he just waved me through. If I had wanted to, I could have easily entered Thailand illegally. However, I needed to get a visa, and didn't fancy risking anything when it came to leaving the country for Malaysia. Once he'd pointed me in the right direction, I convinced him to look after my bike. I discovered I was heading for a *very* long queue.

I joined the queue, but an official soon pulled me out and made me follow him for a few minutes. After ending up back where we started, he handed me a form and told me to fill it in. Following the events in Mumbai airport, I already had a pen to hand and this proved fortunate judging by the number of others I saw fighting over the few that were going round.

After filling out the form, the same guard told me I could jump the queue because I was a foreigner. He then walked off and left me to it. Acting against my British instincts, I took his advice and made my way to the front of the line, where I discovered I wasn't the only one pushing in. It was not civilised in any way, nor was there any subtlety to it. Had I not moved to the front, I would have been there for hours without going anywhere. Using my new-found height advantage, I soon forced my way towards the booth. I had already ridden for eight hours by this point, and I thought my lack of personal hygiene would help me push in. People didn't seem bothered by it though, and one woman (who had pushed in next to me) was especially persistent in trying to elbow me out of the way. Thankfully, there were a number of locals in the queue who seemed to agree with the idea that I should be allowed to the front, so I didn't feel too guilty about disregarding common etiquette. In the end, I was through the border in relatively good time.

When I returned to the man who was minding my bike, he started laughing in genuine amazement that I was back so soon. The whole experience had only taken about half an hour, and I left having enjoyed what was the closest I had come to playing rugby in over six months.

It was a good thing that I didn't enter Thailand without a visa. When I reached the Malaysian border 1,000 miles later, I would have been in a lot of trouble had I turned up without an official stamp allowing me into the country. I had trouble enough as it was.

This time I actively sought out an official to stamp my passport, and yet I was still waved through the Thai side without getting one. When I got to the Malaysian checkpoint, I was forced to turn around again. The bummer was that the Thai checkpoint was at the top of a steep hill and the Malaysian side was at the bottom, so I had to ride back up this road, against one-way traffic. Fun times! When I eventually made it to the top, I noticed a couple of policemen who were obviously a bit perplexed as to why I was going the wrong way through the border. They didn't kick up a fuss, but they watched me all the way until I found and joined the queue I should have been in the first time round.

I got lost trying to find the crossing from Malaysia into Singapore, and was rigorously quizzed when I re-entered the US from Canada, but, other than that, I eventually got the hang of changing nations without incident. Personally, I think that many countries make it far more complicated than it needs to be. Having said that, I have no experience with immigration, so what do I know?

SAFETY

Many people have questioned the safety of my trip, regarding both my personal wellbeing and the possibility of having any important items stolen. I am often asked whether it was dangerous and if I was ever scared.

The simple truth: it was never an issue for me. Road traffic was always going to present a challenge, but that's a slightly different matter, and avoiding those sorts of problems was largely down to me.

In India, I was told by locals that wildlife would be an issue if I camped – so I steered clear of doing so.

In reality, the potential threat envisaged by everyone was that presented by other humans. I actually came back loving humanity. Contrary to what much of the mainstream media preaches, my experiences on this trip showed people everywhere to be amazing, and I never witnessed any malice. There were times when I felt threatened, but most of these were due to my own preconceived ideas and completely unfounded.

The first time I felt genuinely intimidated was in Albania. I was an hour or two outside Tirana, and I'd had to take a detour off the main road. For some reason, there was a two-mile stretch where the road turned into a motorway that I couldn't ride on. I had initially thought I'd be able to make it through regardless, so I ignored the route my dad had set, and carried on past my scheduled turn-off. I soon regretted that decision and had to improvise. I eventually made it on to the correct diversion, but not before I had spent 10 minutes climbing over a roadside barrier and down a steep, muddy bank with my bike.

That minor road led to my first sight of what I regarded as genuine poverty. I don't know why, but I was a bit taken aback to see it in Europe. There was no tarmac on the roads and very little structure to the town, which meant I had to stop to get my bearings.

I was instantly approached by about a dozen curious locals. There were no ill-intentions whatsoever, but my naivety put me on edge, and I made a swift exit. I wasn't rude, but nor did I stick around for an extended chat.

When I reached India a week later, and was confronted with similar or more extreme scenes every five minutes, I was already more relaxed about everything. I have mentioned how difficult it is to get any privacy in India, so if I had felt uneasy about people approaching me, I think I would have had a nervous breakdown. However, one thing I did shy away from was telling people the cost of my bike, particularly in the poorer areas. I was often asked, but never more so than in India. I tried a variety of techniques to direct the conversation elsewhere, from pretending not to understand to saying, "It's a secret."

From my experience, any potential problems seemed more likely in the cities of the developed countries. For example, in the US, I felt distinctly uncomfortable for a lot of the time. I was never actually threatened, but it was in a couple of American cities that I felt most vulnerable. Buffalo was one of these, which I reached after crossing back into the US from Canada and

Niagara Falls. I felt noticeably anxious, and was keen to hurry through it much faster than normal. But, then again, a lot of what I felt may well have been due to my own imagination. I was never actually threatened with violence.

In short, my trip was not completely without danger, but I encountered nothing out of the ordinary and finished with great faith in humanity.

Fast forward two years, and this viewpoint took a bit of a hit. I went on holiday to Thailand with a friend, and, on our first night in Bangkok, we were attacked by a tuk-tuk driver wielding a metal bar. It was the kind of story you hear about, but never think will happen to you. Long story short, he tried to scam us, we said no, we went to get in a different tuk-tuk, and he attacked us. He broke my friend's forearm clean in half and I needed five stitches in my head.

Whilst it makes for a unique holiday anecdote, it put a considerable downer on what was meant to be a diving holiday. The events validated my views on cities being the places to remain cautious, and it unfortunately highlighted the point that there are a few shitty people out there. So, perhaps I was just lucky the first time round. I prefer to think I was unlucky on the second trip.

Anyway, take from that what you will. Overall, safety should not be a major issue, but it only takes one incident, or one person, for things to go wrong. And, if an incident does occur, it can be much harder to remedy when in a foreign country. Even so, there is a lot to be said for making your own luck, so just be sensible and choose your route wisely.

Interesting side note, whilst on the subject of the more recent trip to Thailand: once we finally managed to escape Bangkok, we headed to Koh Tao, which involved a 12-hour bus journey down the east coast. I didn't realise until a couple of hours into the drive, but we were travelling on exactly the same road that I had ridden on for 350 kilometres, two and a half years earlier – the same road that my gear cable snapped on.

Seeing the traffic from inside a bigger vehicle, I can't say that I would want to cycle it again. It didn't faze me at the time, having just finished India, although I can now see why my mum was far from thrilled about the traffic situation when she met me halfway through that stretch.

HUA HIN

When I set off in January, there was a vague plan for my family to come out and meet me in April, so that we could celebrate Anna's 18th birthday together, wherever I happened to be. My initial route had included Cambodia and Vietnam, making Leg 3 Mandalay to Ho Chi Minh. I would then have flown either to Australia or back to Bangkok, and ridden from there to Singapore for Leg 4.

Whilst going through India, this changed. We decided to remove Cambodia and Vietnam from my route, so I instead rode from Mandalay to Singapore, with a five-day stopover in Hua Hin, where I would meet my family.

Hua Hin is just under 200 kilometres south of Bangkok, and this route was far more feasible logistically. However, Cambodia and Vietnam were two countries I had been particularly excited about visiting, so it was a shame to miss them out. Not the end of the world though (pun intended), and it has given me somewhere to go another time.

It took me four days to reach Hua Hin from the Burmese/Thai border. During that time, I experienced my usual mood swings. The third day was a prime example of my fluctuating emotions: I reached my finish point early, and had a decent place to stay, but I was grumpy all evening; for no reason at all.

The five days in Hua Hin were brilliant. It was obviously great to see all my family again, but it was also nice to feel somewhat normal for a short while. I ate huge amounts during my stay and combined it with very little movement. As is always the case, it was over far too quickly. Mum, Dad and Anna had to head back to the UK, and I had to get my legs turning again.

After leaving Hua Hin, it was an 11-day stretch to Singapore via Malaysia. Through previous chapters I have already covered the majority of notable experiences from both Thailand and Malaysia. I had a brief bout of food poisoning before crossing the border, but nothing to the extent of Italy or India. I went into autopilot over this leg, and was constantly fighting fatigue.

So, instead of going into further detail, I will simply include a brief excerpt from the summary on my blog. Reaching Singapore broke the monotony, and I was able to reflect on the previous few weeks with a clearer head:

Southeast Asia has been amazing. The culture obviously takes some getting used to, but, after India, this wasn't a problem. In fact, after leaving India, progressing through Burma, Thailand, Malaysia and now into Singapore, it has become more and more Westernised and easier to handle. For the first time in two months, I can drink the tap water and speak to most people in English, rather than sign language, so this may as well be London!

Flying from Singapore to Perth gave me a complete change of scene and a feeling of rejuvenation.

THE OUTBACK

Landing in Perth was a literal and figurative breath of fresh air. I was able to relax instantly; not least because I was looked after so wonderfully by the Rooney family. (From time to time, I was taken in by various people around the world, and I will talk about all of them a bit later on. I owe a lot of thanks to a lot of people.)

In addition to the brilliant hospitality I received in Perth, the weather, the food, the language and the culture were all familiar. I made a joke about Aussie culture in my blog and I'm led to believe it unintentionally upset a few people:

What's the difference between yoghurt and Australia?
Yoghurt has some culture.

At the time, I think some people misinterpreted this as an unnecessary and uncalled for criticism of the country. That was not the case, so let me set the record straight. I had written a couple of paragraphs in my blog that evening that sounded almost intelligent. I was talking about my feelings, and I thought it was verging on philosophical (it wasn't). Nevertheless, I felt embarrassed posting that online; I didn't feel that I was the teenager who should be engaging in meaningful theories. So, I decided to lower the tone with a joke (something I stated at the time).

I typed *"Australian jokes"* into Google, and that was the first one that made me laugh. I didn't even make it up myself. If you were offended, please consider this a second and genuine apology. I meant nothing by it. It still amuses me though.

There was one other joke that made me laugh. I didn't post it because I wasn't sure everyone would understand it: *"What does a wombat have in common with an Australian bloke? He eats, roots and leaves."*

Anyway, after a relaxing two days in Perth, I set off in a south/ south-westerly direction. As I travelled inland, and further from the coast, I moved further into the bush. With the exceptions of Albany and Esperance, I would argue that I was already in the Outback once I was a mere 300 miles from Perth.

I reached Albany around late morning on Day 76. There, I was met by my friend's aunt (Jen), who bought me breakfast. This was extremely welcome for obvious reasons, but it was also nice to have some human interaction and a normal conversation. That meal was one of the final moments of significant human contact until I was interviewed by a local paper two weeks later.

It was no surprise that I saw fewer people over the next 1,000 miles. Put simply, the Outback is a large expanse of nothing, and makes up a vast proportion of Australia. Within this area is the Nullarbor Plain – a section of desert (arid land, to be specific), located above the Great Australian Bight. It stretches over 750 miles from Norseman to Ceduna, and begins with a sign that reads *"Limited Water. Obtain supplies at Norseman."* There is one road, and on it there are approximately 10 roadhouses, nothing else.

Most of the roadhouses offer somewhere to eat and somewhere to sleep, varying in levels of comfort. I suppose, this is where the Outback 'officially' starts. Even in a car you would sense the remoteness. However, although you get the odd town either side of the Nullarbor itself, they are always at least 70 kilometres apart (often up to 150 kilometres). So, being on a pushbike, I felt as though I was deep into the Outback already before even reaching that point.

It was just after leaving breakfast with Jen, that I joined a road that had a sign saying "*CAUTION – ROAD TRAIN ROUTE*". That was quite indicative, as it emphasised the lack of any other roads. Road trains are very big trucks; the longest routinely used in Australia are approximately 50 metres long. They are certainly not something you want to get hit by – it's bad enough having one drive past you. I received constant warnings about the danger posed by these trucks and their drivers.

It is easy to imagine how someone could lose concentration when driving along arrow-straight roads for hours on end. The common misconception was that the drivers wouldn't notice me until I was plastered across their bonnet. In reality, they all moved over to the opposite lane as they came past, and I think the general public did them a disservice. They only became a real issue when two were coming in opposite directions at the same time, at which point I would opt for a precautionary ride off the tarmac.

Whenever I saw a road train approaching from the front, I would make a point of checking behind me, just in case. I forgot to do this on several occasions though, and was almost caught out a couple of times. The first time, the driver approaching my rear had the courtesy to beep, so that I wouldn't end up as road kill. The second time was closer, and I nearly made a mess in my cycling shorts. The wind was strong at this point, and I couldn't hear the trucks from either direction because of it. I only became aware of the rearward one as it hurtled passed at 60 miles per hour, less than two feet from my bike. I had been utterly clueless up to that point. I would often drift a metre or two into the road whilst my mind wandered, but thankfully I chose not to do it then.

My talk of road trains offered up a new research topic for Chris, and, as ever, his advice was extremely useful:

"As I said earlier, Sara thinks that I should offer you some more useful advice, so I'll do my best. Only this week, I heard from a very unreliable source that truck drivers in Oz are well versed in the art of onanism whilst on the move. Now, fiddling with one's gearstick in the cab of a lorry is rather different to attempting a similar procedure whilst bowling along on your bicycle. And if you are also trying to turn the pages of a magazine or engage with a hot Essex babe on Skype, then it must seem damn near impossible. However, that is what stabilisers are for. They are not, as is widely thought, for teaching children to ride a bike (that would be stupid), but were designed to free up your hands in order to allow the rider to relieve any sexual tension. On the other hand, cycling crushes your nuts and destroys your libido – so you could just use them when you need to tidy up your panniers or check your emails…"

Excluding traffic, signs of life were few and far between in the Outback. Of the people I met, I was surprised to find that they often were not Australian. Quite a few of those working in the petrol stations were actually from the UK, including one Geordie, whose accent gave me quite a surprise.

On Day 76, a few hours after leaving Albany, I reached a place called Wellstead. There, I met a friendly roadhouse owner from

Aberystwyth. He had moved away a long time ago, so no longer had the Welsh accent, but I later realised that Mark Beaumont had written about the same guy in his book (*The Man Who Cycled the World*). I am sure that he's spoken to many cyclists who have gone that way over time. I found it weird to think he would have had a very similar conversation with Beaumont seven years earlier.

The Nullarbor was a surreal but laborious experience. Whilst riding through Europe two months before, Australia – and specifically the desert – had felt far out of reach. I could never comprehend actually getting there, and the feeling never subsided. I never stopped and thought about the fact that every day I was getting closer. When I finally reached Norseman at the start of the Nullarbor, I couldn't quite believe it. It was a huge personal milestone.

The tedium that the Nullarbor presented never bothered me; it was a challenge I welcomed. I was curious about how I would cope with nothing to look at for so many hours. The problem I faced came in the form of a headwind.

I said I would try not to mention the wind too much in this book, but I cannot describe my time on the Nullarbor without doing so. It was seven days across, the first five and a half of which were spent with the wind blowing in my face, and featured the most intense frustration I have ever experienced.

The first day (Day 80), eased me in fairly gently. The wind was far from favourable, but I managed to keep my thoughts positive. The ride that day was 120 miles, with very little climbing, yet it took almost nine hours' riding time.

On the second day, my patience snapped. I had to cross the famous 90-Mile Straight. It's the longest straight road in Australia without even a single kink. I spent every single one of those miles riding directly into the wind:

Today has not been a good one. It started off well with a decent breakfast, but went downhill very rapidly once I started cycling. I've been looking forward to crossing the 90-Mile Straight, but every second of it was unpleasant. The boredom wasn't a problem – the wind was. It was as bad as anything I faced in Europe, and it lasted all day. I also had a bit of grief with my knee early on, and I'm not entirely sure what was causing that.

I can't say much about the ride other than the wind. It was present for every pedal stroke, and, in the final few hours, my frustration started to get the better of me. When I reached the end, I wasn't even relieved; I was just fed up. So, when I walked into the roadhouse and was told that no rooms were available, I had a rather large sense of humour failure. In fact, that's putting it lightly; I pretty much lost the will to live, and sat on the floor next to a petrol pump for 15 minutes trying to sort my head out.

I had three options:

1. Carry on to the next roadhouse (70 kilometres) and decide what to do once there.

2. Set up my tent and try to settle down for the night.

3. Try to get a few hours' sleep in the restaurant of the roadhouse (which is open 24hr) and get moving once rested.

Despite the awful day, I would've gone for the first option if my Garmin hadn't been on the brink of running out of battery. I'm glad I didn't, because that would have been stupid and unnecessary (obviously).

On reflection, the second option was easily the most logical, but it was already very dark and cold, and putting up my tent was not something that appealed to me in the current mindset. I also wanted to get an early start tomorrow, and I knew that packing up the tent in the morning would take time.

So, I decided to give the third option a go. After half an hour and a less-than-acceptable meal, I realised there was no point in not setting up the tent. I had 12 hours until sunrise, and I was not going to spend that in sweaty kit worrying about my bike if I fell asleep.

Putting up the tent was not without difficulties. The ground here is rock solid, so staking it out was impossible. Instead, I've had to tie the corners to my bike and my two panniers in order to prevent it falling over.

I've calmed down a bit now, and I should be able to get some sort of sleep, but today hasn't been great. The wind forecast for tomorrow does not look promising either.

Riding Time: 8:47:04

I hated my tent and, as a result, I very rarely used it, despite carrying it with me for the majority of the 18,000 miles. To save weight, I had bought a small one. The downside was that I couldn't quite sit up in it and I couldn't stretch out in it either if I had any kit inside with me. In hindsight, I should either have opted for a bivvy bag (a very, very small tent) or a bigger, heavier tent that I would have found more comfortable. I tried to find a balance between the two, but instead I ended up with the worst of both.

Europe was too cold to camp – for me anyway – and in India and Southeast Asia I was advised by locals not to do so. This meant that my first night in a tent came on the second day in Australia, and I posted the following thoughts:

I've come to the conclusion that camping is not something I enjoy. It's been an interesting introduction into the life of a tent-dweller, so, in case any of you are unfortunate enough to share a similar experience, I thought I'd offer some advice. If you stay in a campsite and there is an area marked kitchen/BBQ on the map, it's probably just an area to cook your own food, not a restaurant. I didn't realise this, so I'm now off to find some roadkill to put on the campfire.

Condensation is not something I have ever given much thought to, but it's a hot topic amongst campers. I woke up after my first night, surprised to find the inside of my tent soaking wet. I spoke to someone about it at the campsite in the morning. He told me it was normal and there wasn't a whole lot I could do about it.

My next night's camping came two days later at Boxwood Hill. This time, it was not at a campsite, but a petrol station; thankfully, I still had access to a toilet.

I woke up in a tent this morning – so I was about as happy as you'd expect.

I had planned everything slightly better than last time though – by this, I mean I had absolutely everything I needed in my tent. The upside of this being that I didn't need to leave the relative warmth until the last minute. The downside was that I had very little (if any) space to move – so getting ready took a while.

Once on my bike, I felt much better. It's weird to think that cycling 100 miles is the easy part of the day when I camp.

That evening had not been fun, and it presented a new feeling for me. For the first time since the ferry crossing to France, I felt lonely. I'm normally very good at being on my own, and I can have a genuinely enjoyable time with no one but myself for company. It's not often I feel uncomfortable due to being alone. I know a couple of people who are the opposite and who hate being left by themselves. I'm sure to them, this makes me sound a bit strange, so I'd like to point out that I don't have a constant desire to be away from others; I just don't have a problem with it.

I think the feeling of loneliness stemmed from boredom. Usually, I always had something to think about: the next kilometre, the next meal, tomorrow's ride or the amount of sleep I'd get. When I got into my tent that evening, with no phone signal and nothing to do, my thoughts turned to life back home in England. It was not the first time I had felt homesick. Throughout the first couple of months, I would always miss something, whether it was my own bed, my morning cereal or training before work with my best mate. It was the first time I let those thoughts get the better of me though. At that moment, I would have loved to have had someone else with me.

My next camping experience came at the end of the 90-Mile Straight, and it was the final time that I camped in Australia. The later occasions were all in North America. I got better at camping the more I did it. I refined the routine and became more comfortable in my modest quarters. As they say, practice makes perfect, and it was a mistake being so inexperienced before setting off. If I had already known 'how to camp', I suspect I would have used my tent more often.

On my third night of camping, I started to get a grasp on it. I figured out what I needed inside with me, and I slept with the flysheet completely open to prevent condensation. I had a warm sleeping bag, so this seemed to be the best option. I encountered a slight issue with this method in Canada when it started raining, but I'll talk about that later.

Day 3 on the Nullarbor was more of the same, and, with nothing to look at, I resorted to alternative ways of distracting myself. At one stage, I shouted continuous expletives at the wind for a good 10 minutes. It helped my mood, but I stopped when my throat started to hurt. This was also one of the few occasions I talked to myself. I would always think aloud, something I still do (it's a difficult habit to break), but, here, I actively had a conversation with myself as a distraction. It didn't last very long. I was only partially mad and still very much aware that I was conversing with myself. It was mainly an experiment to gauge my sanity.

The fourth day was another case of wind rage, and the only break from my purgatory was meeting a 79-year-old man called Douglas. He was cycling in the opposite direction, but riding around the coast of Australia (12,500 miles) for the fifth time in nine years. I thought that was awesome.

Day 5 on the Nullarbor was hard. It was the longest day of the whole trip, in terms of actual riding time (although not mileage), and I felt it. An accumulation of the previous day's workload meant that I started off tired. Riding into those winds, I was working harder than normal, but averaging around 20 km/h. For the same effort with no wind, I would have been travelling at around 27–30 km/h. This is where my frustration came from. I knew how much effort I was putting in, yet I was getting nowhere. Not only that, but, given the distances I was covering, this added over two hours per day to my time in the saddle.

I reached my finishing point, after 122 miles and 9 hours and 35 minutes of riding, with my legs completely spent. Excluding the extreme days where other factors were in play – like the heat in Burma – that was the most physically drained I felt at the end of a day. For any cycling enthusiasts, although I didn't have a power meter, I would wager that day produced the highest training stress score (TSS) of any day on my trip. On top of the obvious things, such as the distance and the wind, there were other things to contend with. For days, whenever I stopped for a rest or something to eat, there would be nowhere to sit down, and I would end up either standing or sitting on the stony ground. It may seem trivial, but, when even your rests are uncomfortable, it makes everything exponentially worse.

When standing, your legs don't recover. When sitting on stone, your arse doesn't recover, and if you are as inflexible as I am, sitting on the floor is never comfy at the best of times. My arse was a *tender* subject, and something I was frequently asked about.

Obviously, it became a tad fragile. There was the odd day where I struggled to get comfortable on the bike, but, thankfully, I never had any major problems (i.e. large saddle sores). I was very wary of this being a possibility, so I was vigilant about taking precautions. Firstly, I bought a good saddle. I went for a Brooks Cambium C17, which is made of vulcanised rubber – it has no padding, but some flexibility. As it happens, I bought mine very soon after the model was released. So, by the end of my trip, it is likely that I had ridden that type of saddle further than anyone else in the world. An interesting statistic, which I realised whilst riding across the Nullarbor.

In addition to the saddle, I made a concerted effort to wash my shorts every night, and was always liberal with the 'chammy' (chamois) cream when setting off in the morning. I also made use of some pawpaw cream in the evening (which acts as a healing agent). I could go into more detail, but I appreciate that may be too much information for some. So, in answer to those many questions: yes, of course my arse hurt – that's going to happen if you spend the average person's working day on a saddle. Thankfully, I never encountered anything I couldn't grit my teeth through though.

Perhaps I owe Chris some thanks for this; early on in my trip, he shared yet more valuable advice. Not being a cyclist, I can't imagine how he came by this worldly knowledge:

"When putting on chamois cream, never look anyone in the eye. It's awkward, especially for non-cyclists, who have no idea what you're doing. To them you just look creepy. Also be aware that we all have a certain face we make when we're putting our hand down our shorts to apply chamois cream. Try looking in the mirror sometime during application – you might find you have a bit of a scary 'O' face!

"After sticking your hand down your pants with a handful of chamois cream and rubbing it around a bit, do not touch anything until you wash your hands. Don't rub the residual cream on your legs and call it good. Don't touch your bike. Most definitely don't reach for food or your drink bottle. Your chamois hand is contaminated and should be quarantined until it is disinfected!!!

"Better still – avoid all this nonsense and travel by taxi."

He had a point. The problem with cycling is that it's not just your legs and your bum that hurt; it's everything. I've mentioned the issues I had with my knee (and even my tongue in Burma), but these were exceptions that I would not ordinarily consider to be part of cycling. However, even without taking it to idiotic extremes, cycling can be an uncomfortable sport. I have always suffered as a result, particularly with my back and neck. Then there are parts which only flare up on occasion, often on the longer rides – your hands, feet and arms. As I reached the latter stages of Europe and at the beginning of India, I realised these minor aches and pains were going to become part of the daily grind.

My hands only started hurting about a week into India, after I had made it through Europe and sent the thick gloves home with my other winter gear. Over the following months, my hands toughened up, but by America I had permanent bruises on my palms from the constant pressure. With only three places to distribute your bodyweight on a bike (hands, feet and bum), I suppose it has to be expected. What I had not realised was that it would also affect my fingers. By the end of the trip, I had no feeling in the tips of either of my third and fourth fingers. Thankfully, this was not permanent, but it took a few months for the odd sensation to disappear. At the time, I didn't think about it. It didn't affect my riding, so there was nothing to be done. When I reached Thailand, I double-wrapped my bar tape to add some extra padding, but that was as much as I could do.

My feet were worse. When your hands start to ache, it's relatively simple to change position on the handlebars to ease the pressure, but when your feet start to ache, there's not a whole lot that can be done except grimace. All these little things add up, and they can be difficult to ignore when you are in a desert with nothing else to think about.

Featuring a lot of these pains, my penultimate morning on the Nullarbor was just as shit as the preceding days. Mercifully, the wind and my fortunes changed to carry me through the final day and a half, to the end of the Nullarbor in Ceduna.

I didn't mind the emptiness that the desert offered. I had set out to push myself mentally, and dealing with boredom is a big part of that. Had it not been for the wind, I would have enjoyed the Nullarbor. Instead, I hated it with every fibre of my being. Even more irritatingly, the prevailing wind should have been a tailwind, and the following week it changed and started blowing the other way. Typical.

MIND GAMES

I never used headphones when riding my bike. I wrote about my stance on the matter in my blog, the day I reached Ceduna. Here is that entry:

Apart from "Why are you doing this?", the question I get asked the most is whether I listen to music whilst cycling. The answer is no. Before setting off, if you'd asked me, I may have said, "No, but I might do across the desert." Well, in case anyone was wondering – I have now crossed the desert, and I didn't. There are a number of reasons why not, including the fact that it makes it easier. Personally, I don't think one should be deprived of the mental challenge that comes with cycling. One of the main reasons I'm doing this trip is to push myself, both mentally and physically, so to listen to music would almost feel like cheating.

The other reason may make slightly more sense, and it is probably the one I should lead with when answering this question. Whilst riding, our eyes and ears are what prevent us from crashing (assuming you have mastered the balancing part). That being said, most of the time, one's eyes are looking forward, and therefore our ears are the only things that will warn us of something dangerous approaching from the rear. Here is a list of a few things you DO want to hear before they reach your rear wheel:

Another cyclist: If they're behind you, you want to keep them back there. It's a bit late to up the pace once they've already overtaken you.

A monkey: Believe me, if a monkey starts chasing you, you will know about it. So, it's better that the realisation comes before it's biting at your calves.

A dog: Same reason as the monkey, although slightly more frequent and slightly less terrifying... unless it's an Albanian dog, in which case it may as well be a bear.

A road train: For obvious reasons, you do not want to be caught out by one of these, especially if it's travelling across the Nullarbor carrying a portacabin that hangs three-feet over the edge on both sides. A pre-emptive ride into a ditch is not always the worst outcome.

Anyway, that's my long-winded answer to a rather simple question.

Cycling is a sport steeped in tradition, and, as such, it has many unwritten rules. Ironically, there is a book that covers most of these (written by the Velominati, and aptly named *The Rules*). Whilst the book is based on truth, it is a humorous look into the history and traditions of cycling, and should *not* be taken too seriously. There are those who will follow its teachings to the letter and chastise those that do not. These people should be ignored and left to their pretentious ways. My advice to any new cyclists: enjoy the book – it's funny – but, more importantly, enjoy riding your bike.

Some rules may seem superficial, but these are often the more necessary ones. This includes "*Rule #37 – The arms of the eyewear shall always be placed over the helmet straps.*" This is just the way it is, don't fight it. Other rules, such as "*No food on training rides under 4 hours*", should be taken with a pinch of salt. Unless you are still living in the 1980s, this is a good one to ignore.

Anyway, Rule #62 states "*You shall not ride with earphones.*" The reasons listed in the book align closely with what I wrote in my blog. Despite this, I actually have my own reasons for leaving the music at home, and they are not all in line with what *The Rules* says.

There are several practical safety reasons for keeping your ears free, but, truthfully, you can quite easily ride without bumping into things, even when listening to music. Therefore, unless it's a group ride, I have no problem with others using headphones. I don't do it, purely because I don't want to rob myself of the sport I fell in love with. I was once watching a video on YouTube about a CrossFit athlete from Finland, named Mikko Salo. In the video, he says something to the effect of, "If you need music to work out, you need to find a new hobby." I agree with that wholeheartedly.

I do not like running; I get bored stupid when I do it, and I listen to music as a way of avoiding the boredom. That's not always the case if I'm somewhere like the Alps, where the views can serve as distraction enough, but my point is that I don't face the same problem with cycling. I was worried that if I started to ride with music, I would become dependent on it. I was afraid that my feelings for cycling might drift towards that of running.

Secondly, this trip was largely about the mental battle. If my body had failed me, I would have been disappointed, but not angry. If my mind had failed me, if I had lacked the necessary mental toughness, I would have hated myself. I was there to push my limits, and I wasn't going to do that by distracting my brain with music or an audiobook. Something I did contemplate was to listen to a language-learning tape, as that would have been genuinely productive, but this notion was also discarded.

As a disclaimer, I do listen to music when I'm training on the turbo (indoor bike). It increases performance, and there is a limit to my masochism.

With all that being said, if not music, what did I think about? I needed some way to keep my mind occupied. It was an art I learnt to perfect throughout the trip, and I eventually reached a point where I could 'zone out' and ponder almost nothing.

Usually, whilst out on a normal ride at home, if boredom takes hold I resort to increasing the intensity and converting the boredom into pain: swapping one evil for another. Unfortunately, this wasn't much of an option with the situation I found myself in. Although I often did so, whenever I decided to increase the pace, it would come back to bite me the next day. When riding for days on end, a steady pace is the best option.

In short, I was very bored a lot of the time – especially through Europe at the start. The countryside was cold and empty, and I was new to the solitude. I spent many hours obsessively going over the numbers on my Garmin. Constantly looking at my speed, time, distance to go; calculating when I would arrive and working out how much time I would save if I sped up by a specific amount. Converting kilometres to miles, and miles to kilometres. Essentially, I spent a large portion of my time doing mental arithmetic and worrying about how much sleep I would get that night. It was still exceedingly boring, but it was a way of maintaining what little sanity I had.

When I reached India, boredom was not so much of a problem. The weather helped my general mood, but I was also fascinated by everything that I saw. I didn't always have a great time riding through India, it was often a real pain in the backside, but boredom was rarely an issue. That was until food poisoning struck, with four days to go. Feeling as bad as I did, I couldn't focus on anything. I couldn't move my head without a wave of nausea washing over me. So, I kept my eyes glued forwards. Even the numbers ticking over on my Garmin made me feel sick, so I hid it in my back pocket. I could do nothing but wallow in self-pity and embrace the tedium.

Those few days were horrendous, amongst the worst I had, but they taught me a crucial skill: I learnt to zone out. I learnt to let my mind go blank, and not rely on the numbers, the scenery or the people to keep me entertained. I realised the key did not lie in finding something to keep my mind working, it was all about accepting the fact that my mind would not be working.

Whilst riding through the dull expanse of northern France, I tweeted about how there was absolutely nothing to look at. I received a reply from a guy who had just finished cycling around the world himself. It read something along the lines of, "*If you're bored already, wait till you get to the desert!*" The truth is, when I finally reached the desert, boredom wasn't a problem; I had a handle on it by then.

To illustrate this, I remember everything from Europe. My emotions were running high, I was constantly on edge and always focused. As a consequence, every day, every hotel and every meal stuck in my head. I can recall the majority of most days. The same cannot be said for the later stages of the trip. As I began to master the art of letting my mind wander, the days blurred into one, and I began to forget the details. Looking back on North America, there are stretches of up to three days where I find it difficult to evoke anything significant, even when reading back over my blog.

Whilst it would be nice to remember everything about the experience, there were very long stretches of not very much, so it isn't surprising. Plus, being able to detach my mind from my legs was imperative.

Pro Tip: letting your mind drift is essential for your sanity. However, it is important not to let it drift too far. I found myself riding off the road a number of times when I lost so much concentration that I came close to falling asleep as well. Generally, I would receive only a sharp awakening from the sudden change in road surface. One dodgier occasion came in Burma (Day 55). It was the second time that day I had strayed from the road, but this time there was drop of about half a metre from the tarmac to the dirt on the side. I'm not entirely sure how I stayed upright, nor how I let myself become so unaware. It could have been much worse, so, take it from me, be careful when sliding in and out of dreams on a bike.

HALFWAY

On Day 87, the day following the Nullarbor stretch, I finished in a place called Port Kenny. I had covered around 8,865 miles in total by then. I was 146 miles from Port Lincoln (the next place that I would be able to get a room for the night), and 565 miles from Adelaide.

I had arranged to stay the night with friends in Adelaide six days later and to ride out of the city with a small group the following day. The prospect of riding with others was something I was really looking forward to and not something I wanted to miss out on.

My original plan had been to ride 100 miles on Day 88, pitch a tent, then have a short Day 89, where I would stop in Port Lincoln. This would leave me with four days to cover 420 miles to Adelaide, so it would all work out nicely.

The objection I had to this plan was the involvement of another night in my tent, which was something I had quickly developed a strong dislike for. I therefore went to bed, partially considering riding the 146 miles to Port Lincoln the next day. I knew I was physically capable, but it was a bit unnecessary, and would no doubt have a negative effect on the following days.

I was woken in the morning by the wind blowing a gale outside. I had grown to hate the notion of any kind of wind, but, when I looked out the window to see a cloudless sunrise and the trees bending in the right direction, I knew I was on for a good day.

Once I was on the bike, I remained conservative with my ambitions, and kept the idea of Port Lincoln in the back of my mind. I decided not to put any pressure on myself and just see how things went. I reached my planned camping spot at 1.30pm, so there was no way I was stopping there. I let my parents know the change of plan and carried on my way.

This change put me a day ahead of schedule, and was the reason I was able to take a day off in Adelaide. Just under three hours later, I hit the 9,000-mile mark – halfway around the world. It was a huge milestone to reach, and even better that it came when I was already in a good mood. It was an unassuming location about 20 kilometres outside Port Lincoln, but it meant a lot to me.

My mentality changed there and then. From that point on I had already ridden further than what was left to do, and I knew I was capable.

It's funny how big a part the mind plays in a trip like this. Despite knee problems, illness, adverse weather, etc., the hardest aspect to contend with was the concept of riding almost every day for six months.

The moment I hit 9,000 miles, it changed. It was like flicking a switch. Having three months left on the road still scared me, but, when it came to the distance, I had a reference point. It was what I had just done. And, in theory, the half I had left would be easier due to the countries I would be riding through. Most used the English language and had slightly more favourable climates. Luckily, this proved to be true – although only marginally.

I was feeling amazing by the time I reached Port Lincoln. I had just ridden my longest day of the trip, and, honestly, I wasn't even that tired. Perhaps it was adrenaline, but I felt as though I could have done another four hours without any trouble. I also had two interviews that evening, which was pretty cool for timing. One was for the local newspaper (*The Port Lincoln Times*) and the other was a radio interview, in which the radio presenter compared my accent to Prince Harry's. It made me laugh, but, I must stress, there are no similarities.

I am regularly asked about my longest day, but, in truth, I never aimed to achieve a ridiculous daily distance. I knew I would be riding the next day, so it was unnecessary. In any event, the big mileage days aren't the ones that make the difference. Mark Beaumont expressed this well: *"People always talk about the massive days, the 230-mile days* [admittedly I never did one that long], *but records are really set on the 80-mile days, when I have food poisoning, the bike is breaking and I am left carrying it through mud."*

This was not a sentiment I considered at the time, mind you, and I went to sleep in Port Lincoln feeling unusually pleased with myself. Predictably, I was promptly knocked off my high horse the next morning, because I managed to lock myself out of my room for 45 minutes. I had gone outside to check the weather and shut my door with the key inside. I then had to wait until someone with a spare key showed up. Thankfully, I had at least taken the decision to put some clothes on first.

FAMILY DOWN UNDER

On Day 93, I rode out of Adelaide with four other guys. I had a half-day planned, and was due to stop at Murray Bridge, just 50 miles away. Despite being extremely wet, that ride was awesome. Not only was the extra company a welcome change, but I glimpsed the cycling terrain that Adelaide is famous for. It was a shame about the weather; I caught it on one of the worst days of the year, apparently. Regardless, it didn't prevent me noticing that Adelaide should be high up on everyone's places-to-go-with-a-bike list.

That evening, I met up with Ray and Steve. Ray is Dad's uncle, Steve is Ray's son, and therefore Dad's cousin – as is Richard, who would join us a few days later. They were to stay with me for the ensuing week (travelling in a car), and it was brilliant being with family.

The first day they joined me, I set their expectations pretty low by getting two punctures. The first wasn't my fault; the second was due to the same piece of metal as the first, and was therefore mostly my fault.

The following few days were great. It was the same principle as when Dad joined me in the south of France – having company made an immeasurable difference. Not only did every aspect of the day become easier, but it also became enjoyable. Just having people there to talk to and have a laugh with was something I didn't realise I was missing until then. The only bummer was the weather, which remained wet for a lot of that period.

We spent our first night in a town called Keith. Its main/only tourist attraction is a 'Land Rover on a pole'. On one website, it is listed as one of Australia's worst tourist attractions. I didn't even bother looking for it. After a further two days' riding through wine country, Richard joined us at the end of Day 96. Steve had to leave the next morning, unfortunately, but I would meet back up with him after Melbourne.

Day 97 was one of my favourites of the whole trip. Although the first quarter of the day's 208 kilometres was fairly windy and uneventful, after that I reached the Great Ocean Road – which is absolutely stunning. I was there in bad weather, and I was still blown away by it. It is, hands down, my favourite road of the trip. I have had the luxury of riding on numerous Alpine climbs that are any cyclist's dream, and I think the Great Ocean Road still surpasses them in many ways. The views are sublime, the road surface is smooth, and the traffic is bearable. I'm not a motorcyclist, but I can imagine it being a perfect destination for them as well. I didn't even see the Twelve Apostles, which I'm sure, on their own, would be a selling point for many.

The Twelve Apostles are a collection of stone stacks just off the shore. There are now only eight left, although I'm led to believe that there were only ever nine (don't quote me on that). Unfortunately, you can't quite see them from the road, and it would have added at least half an hour if I had made the detour.

With a fair distance still to go, and sunset fast approaching, I decided against it. Honestly, I don't feel like I've missed out at all – the coast road was stunning all the way along.

Enter Chris:

"What sort of travel writer are you? Every time there is something interesting nearby you tell us that you missed it and it probably wasn't worth it anyway!!! If you can't get hold of this stuff why are you there? Strewth… come on, fella, up your game."

Earlier that morning, we had discussed where to stop for the night; we could either stay in Port Campbell after 160 kilometres, or Lavers Hill after 208 kilometres. The latter was made even more of an effort as it sat at the top of a 20-kilometre climb. The dismal weather was making the decision more difficult, but, in order to stay on target for hitting Bairnsdale (Steve's home town) three days later, we opted to aim for the further distance. And I am so glad that we did.

The last two hours of that day remain some of the best I've ever had on a bike. The ride beforehand had already been good. The Great Ocean Road served as the perfect respite for my tired head. As the sun started to set, the road headed uphill, and the rain became more persistent.

Richard drove ahead with Ray to check into the motel, and I was left to my usual isolation. Alone with the sound of my breathing, the light from my head torch illuminating little more than the rain drops in front of my face, I found myself in absolute bliss. I suppose it could be a weird concept for non-cyclists or non-sportspeople to understand. The idea that you can feel good, whilst simultaneously experiencing a significant amount of pain and discomfort.

That climb up to Lavers Hill was my favourite of the whole trip. I don't remember anything significant; I just remember feeling incredible. My legs felt alive for the first time in weeks, as if I'd somehow shaken the underlying and ever-present fatigue. In that moment, any thoughts going around my head faded, and I focused on nothing but pushing my legs onwards.

The second half of the Great Ocean Road, whilst it lacked the surreal experience of the evening before, was equally stunning. I finished the day in Queenscliffe – at the bottom of Port Phillip (Melbourne) Bay – very happy indeed. I caught a ferry across the bay the next morning, but, unfortunately, this was where I left Richard and Ray. I met Steve again on the other side of the crossing, and he stayed with me for the next two days to Bairnsdale, where I had another day off – this time with Steve and some of his family.

I reached Bairnsdale after 100 days' riding, so it was a nice round number to stop on. Steve, Leanne (Steve's wife) and Sam (one of their four children) looked after me for the day. This included showing me an island full of koalas, which was cool. They also kept me fully satisfied on the food front, which was no mean feat!

Inevitably, and all too soon, I had to get back on my bike, and, after five wet, hilly days, I reached Sydney. It's easy to gloss over stretches like this in my head, because I was between two significant milestones that were relatively close together. In reality, those five days still meant riding 500 miles. They also contained a surprising amount of climbing, and one of them was the wettest day I'd had since Europe, so they were far from straightforward.

On the last of those days, I met some more family friends, who escorted me into the city, and then I met up with my cousin Stephanie and her now-husband, Doug. They had me to stay for the following day and showed me around Manly; I would thoroughly recommend a visit. I loved it there. It was another rare occasion where I did things normal people would do, such as go for a walk, look in shops and chill out. It was fun.

I received a fantastic farewell from Abbotsleigh School when I left the city the next day. My former primary-school music teacher, who now teaches in Sydney, had organised for the school to come out and cheer me on as I rode past. I was utterly stunned, and I must say a huge thanks to Stephan and everyone there. From what I gather, getting the whole school out of lessons at the right time proved a logistical nightmare for both Stephan and my mum, who was coordinating with him.

My final six days to Brisbane involved a lot of climbing. Dad and I had decided, at fairly short notice, that it would be best to avoid the busy coast road. Instead, I headed inland over the Great Dividing Range. We drastically misjudged how 'great' this dividing range was. It wasn't quite the Alps, but it was big enough to present a distinct drop in temperature, a significant amount of climbing and regular sense of humour failures from yours truly. As if to hammer home this routing error, one local said to me, "Huh… You've chosen a weird part of the country to cycle through." As if I hadn't already noticed.

On the plus side, I felt as though I had achieved something when I arrived in Brisbane on Day 111. Even without cycling the rest of Australia, the last bit from Sydney was enough to be pleased about.

BIKE SHOPS

Excluding the wheel problems that I had in North America, I was very fortunate when it came to mechanical issues. Part of it was luck, part of it was starting off with good equipment (thanks to Condor) and part of it came down to the fact that I regularly had the bike checked by mechanics more competent than me. On a couple of occasions, my bike was saved just when it was on the brink of a major failure.

The first significant stop – Istanbul – was only 2,500 miles into my travels, and everything was still running smoothly. So, other than a change of tyres, it didn't need much done. Dad and I cleaned it (he did most of it), but there was no need for a new chain or cassette.

India was a similar story. By this point, the bike had done 5,000 miles, and, whilst it was still fully functional, it could have done with a few new components. My dad, who was flying to meet me in Kolkata, asked our contact there to book it into a bike shop for a quick service. I laughed when I heard this because I knew exactly what was coming. Having not been to India before, I don't think Dad had appreciated the differences between a bike shop in London and a 'bike shop' in Kolkata. I didn't say anything at first, in the hope that I would be proved wrong. I wasn't.

We turned up to a dusty shack in the middle of a bustling Kolkata market. I had spent three weeks in India and had never encountered anything more than this in terms of a bike shop. Dad was slightly taken aback. Neither of us were sure whether my bike would leave in a better condition than it went in.

We spent the best part of the next hour exploring the rest of the market. One stall was selling chicken meat. The chickens were all kept in cages at the back of the stall, and one of the guys was 'transforming' them from live chickens to pieces of meat that you could cook. It took him about a minute to turn a live bird into breast, wings and legs – all completely plucked. He made it look effortless, and it was oddly mesmerising to watch.

Upon returning to my bike, I was happy to see that whilst little had improved, no harm had been done. When my gear cable snapped in Thailand two weeks later, it was a nice surprise to find a 21st-century bike shop that would sort everything out for me. The shop was of a standard that wouldn't have looked out of place in central London and went by the imaginative name of Hua Hin Bikes. If you're looking for a bike shop in Hua Hin, it's the one run by a very friendly, but rather loud, old lady.

We decided my drivetrain was already fairly knackered, but thought we may as well wait until Singapore to change it. The gear cables were obviously replaced and also the handlebar tape, which had become one of the most unpleasant smelling things in the entire country. It's often customary for bike shops to give your old parts back to you. When we went to pick my bike up, I was not expecting to receive my old bar tape back in a plastic bag. We didn't have the heart to tell them to bin it themselves. It would have stunk out the whole shop.

My next stop was in Singapore. Obviously, it is a major city with lots to choose from, so we worked off a recommendation from Alex (a cycling mate from London, who was living in Singapore) and went to one called T3 Bicycle Gears Bike shop. They replaced the whole drivetrain and even the bar tape again, which had already started to unravel. I asked the bike shop to double-wrap it this time to give my hands extra padding. That bar tape is still on the bike at the time of writing. It's arguably a tad unhygienic, but I've washed it thoroughly a number of times and it hasn't started to smell again (yet). I think India was largely to blame for that happening the first time round. I received fantastic hospitality at T3 from Jim and Mel, and they even gave me some freebies, including a couple of cycling jerseys.

The next set of repairs worth mentioning was in Brisbane. I'd had a brief service in Adelaide, but nothing too dramatic. By Brisbane, my bike had done over 4,000 miles since Singapore, and needed some attention. I was taken by Dominic O'Sullivan (who was letting me stay with him and his family) to his friend Ben at Hola Cycles. I cannot thank Ben enough. It was a Saturday afternoon, I was flying to New Zealand the next morning, and I came in unannounced with a messed-up bike. He dropped everything and immediately went to work, whilst I left to get some physio treatment. About 45 minutes later, I got a call from Ben telling me that he had taken out the bottom bracket and a load of water had poured out – not ideal.

I didn't return to the shop because I was getting treatment on my knee and was under time constraints. Dom picked up my bike for me, and Ben had given it a full service, including a new bottom bracket, all for free. I never got the chance to say thank you in person, let alone actually try to pay for his services. Ben, I would love to buy you a beer or two if you are ever in London!

After an uneventful, but perfectly adequate service in Auckland, my next stop was the unplanned one in Portland when my wheel broke. I have already touched on this, although another thank you to Kyle and Showers Pass is due.

After that, it was Niagara Falls, which turned into a bit of a nightmare. I cannot remember the name of the place I went to – if I could, I would urge anyone to steer clear of it. The bloke in there talked a good game, but managed to lose one of the spacers in my cassette and left my bike in a worse condition than when it went in.

I finished in Boston four days after that and then flew to Lisbon, where I had a new wheel (and cassette) waiting for me. This wheel was from Condor, who deserve the biggest mention. They built my bike to begin with, offered amazing support throughout, and I could not have asked for any more from them – apart from a free bike I suppose.

NEW ZEALAND

New Zealand was the least challenging stretch of the trip. That is not to say it was easy. I went into it with only one day off after a long Australian leg, my knee was playing up and it was heading into winter. On paper, it could have been really shit. However, having Dad join me in a car made all the difference.

We were lucky with the weather, which made a welcome change. It was still cold, and it rained a fair amount, but we avoided any snow, and the temperature was never far below 0°C. On top of that, we had a narrow escape in Dunedin; two days after we left, the city was flooded with over a foot of water.

The good fortune regarding the weather was nice, but not essential. Even if it had snowed, New Zealand would have remained a relative breeze. Dad was able to put both my panniers in the car, so I was lugging around far less weight than normal. Not only did this mean I was able to ride a bit faster, it also eased the strain on my knee. The injury was still there, but the feeling subsided to an annoyance, rather than genuine pain. Having someone to nag me in the evenings about stretching also helped.

The real benefit of having some company is in the mental side of things. I didn't have to think about anything other than riding my bike over those days, with the exception of writing my blog in the evenings. The experience was representative of the 'marginal gains' philosophy, something that is now prominent in all high-level sport. Improve every aspect of your day, even by the tiniest amount, and all those small changes will accumulate to have a big effect. It's not something I was ever particularly focused on, but, in hindsight, it's clear to see how much of a difference it made. Simple tasks, such as packing in the morning, deciding when and where to get food, and drying my kit overnight, all ceased to be an issue. It made the world of difference. My dad made New Zealand enjoyable for me.

I started cycling when I was 14 because of him, and I fell in love with it a year later when we cycled from London to Chamonix (in the French Alps) together. None of my close mates cycled, so I spent many of my favourite teenage hours out on the bike with Dad.

I often get asked why I did this trip solo. Part of the reason is that I would have had to find someone of equal ability. I would not have wanted to be held up by anyone, and I would have hated it even more if I was the limiting factor in the partnership. The main reason though – of the people I knew that cycled, there were only two that I would genuinely want to spend that much time with. My cousin Henry, who is the closest I have to a brother, and my dad.

I won't go into too much detail, because I don't think I could do any kind of justice to the feelings I have for Dad. The fact that I burst into tears when I saw him on the Turkish border should serve as evidence of this. In short, there is no one I would rather have spent those 12 days in New Zealand with.

Had I not had the company, New Zealand might have been slightly underwhelming. The scenery was decent, but I avoided the more picturesque west coast because of snow and the mountains. The roads were also disappointing. They were deceptively rough, and I had a constant buzz going through my body. The truth is, nothing overly exceptional happened in New Zealand, I was just going through the motions and sticking to my routine.

However unexceptional it may have been, there were still many brilliant moments. One being the discovery of a particularly fantastic road sign.

Place names and amusing road signs provided brief mental respite throughout the whole trip. It started in Slovenia. I was only there for a few hours, but the snow, wind and hills made me so miserable that I resorted to reading their road signs aloud for amusement. I have rarely been so interested in something quite so dull.

Things became more interesting once I reached the southern hemisphere, and I started my own 'favourite sign' contest. Australia kicked things off with some weird and wonderful names, including Nowhere Else, Salmon Gums, Grass Patch, Cocklebiddy, Widgiemooltha and Potato Point. The last of which prompted me to write one of the stranger paragraphs in my blog:

The sun eventually broke through the clouds and turned the middle section of today into a very nice ride. About the same time, I passed a sign for "Potato Point". I didn't actually go through it, but it made me wonder why on earth anyone would name a place after a vegetable. I mean it's not like you can drive around England and spot signs for "Broccoli-upon-Avon" or "Sutton and Eggplant". That's what went through my head whilst riding anyway; I'm not entirely sure it's relevant now, but you get the idea.

When I first saw the sign I had a very irrational rant to myself. I then spent the next half an hour coming up with Broccoli-upon-Avon, and Sutton and Eggplant. I guess whatever it takes to keep yourself interested, although I don't know why my thoughts ran to eggplant: being British, I'd normally call it an aubergine.

Moving away from the weird-sounding names, I arrived at the more puerile and childish ones. Iron Knob replaced Widgiemooltha as my favourite when I happened upon it, although Blackbutt – also in Australia – gave it a run for its money. North America provided some good ones in the form of Fort Dick, Grassy Knob, Fluckinger and Bismarck. My dad also took great pleasure in notifying me whenever I would be riding through somewhere with 'Beaver' in the name – of which there were many. I suspect he enjoyed Big Beaver Creek the most.

My favourite of all came on the first day of New Zealand. I had seen it on the map so even had my camera at the ready when I rode past the sign: "*Shag Point*". Brilliant. Why beat around the bush with subtle connotations? If you happen to have a local dogging site, why not advertise it? If you want to make a bored cyclist happy, change your local town sign to something rude. Or draw something rude on it – I saw a lot of that too.

But, I digress. I shall now include a few excerpts of my blog from the New Zealand leg:

Day 113 – *Timaru to Christchurch*

Unfortunately, today was not that exciting. I spent the day on a busy and mostly flat road. The views of yesterday didn't feature, and I spent the majority of the latter half riding into the wind.

Apart from that, it was fine. Having my dad with me makes things considerably easier, and I've had a very relaxed evening without any of the usual stress. I even fell asleep before dinner, which is not something I've done on many occasions.

The only real talking point of today is that I cycled over New Zealand's longest bridge, which was about as impressive as Manu Tuilagi's disciplinary record.

Day 118 – New Plymouth to Te Kuiti

It turns out I hit 12,000 miles at the end of yesterday, and I didn't realise until this morning. (That's two-thirds of 18,000 for those not so mathematically gifted). Reaching this milestone has had an even bigger mental effect than reaching halfway. The end suddenly feels much closer than it should. After Auckland, I only have two legs left (the US and Europe), and I think that's making it sound easier than it is. I'm close to finishing New Zealand, but that's a mental state I need to stay away from. The reality of 6,000 miles will no doubt catch back up soon.

Today has been good in general. My legs showed glimpses of yesterday's form but were mostly turning over at their normal pace. The scenery today was good though, so the hills and lack of speed didn't bother me that much.

We're now staying in Te Kuiti, which is apparently the sheep-shearing capital of the world! At least I think they said shearing...

I have read over my blog, but can think of little else to say about New Zealand. I had four days riding in the South Island, one day crossing between the Islands and five days riding to Auckland in the North Island. Despite the limited excitement, I enjoyed myself and it served as an important part of my journey; not least because those days marked the last for my beard, which I had been growing since Perth (two months earlier). I had grown it purely out of principle. I hated it, but it seemed like the right thing to do considering the adventurous nature of what I was attempting. In hindsight, I should have kept it for America. It's not as if I needed to impress anyone, and it might have fooled people into thinking I was over 21 so I could have a beer.

In riding through New Zealand, I entered the final third of my journey. It was a big milestone and it made the finish feel tangible, even if there were still 6,000 miles to go. I also ticked off my first antipodal point in Wellington. As per Guinness World Records, to officially cycle round the world, I had to pass through two antipodal points – two points on opposite sides of the Earth. Mine were Wellington and a place near Valladolid in the middle of Spain. Chris – unsurprisingly – interpreted the term in a different way:

"I am stunned – and also a tad confused. I had always thought that the antipodal point was something in the rectal passage. I say this because I am sure at my last medical, the doctor spent a long time with a rubber glove on looking for it. Mind you, I suppose that type of examination is still covered by the phrase 'down under'…"

THE US OF A

Land of the free, and the home of some absolute nutcases. I saw a sign across someone's field in Montana that read: *"Pray and you'll meet God, trespass and you'll meet him sooner"*. Make of that what you will; I laughed when I saw it, but I don't think it reflects a positive side of the country.

I am going to be very upfront and let you know from the outset that I am going to slate the US. Save for a couple of aspects, I hated the place, so if this is going to offend you, perhaps just skip to the next chapter.

Of course, I didn't hate everything about the country, but when I reached San Francisco five months into my trip, I was already desperate to get home. At the time, this made me hypercritical of everything, so my views are definitely biased. I did have some amazing experiences, rode through some amazing places and met some amazing people, but in this chapter, I am going to focus on some of the things I disliked.

Why? I get asked a lot about the US and my thoughts towards it. I get the impression people want to hear my honest answer. I could be wrong, but you have read this far, so I figure I'll keep going…

Things that annoyed me:
- The food. It is generally shite. Really, really shite.
- The drinking age. I could cycle across the whole sodding continent (literally), but not enjoy a beer in the evenings. I could own a gun and still not have a beer!
- The gun laws. Seriously WTF!?
- Unfounded patriotism.
- The tipping culture.
- Political correctness.
- They say things incorrectly.
- Donald Trump. He wasn't such an issue whilst I was there, but he is now adding to my list of reasons not to go back.

Things I enjoyed:
- My accent. Being surrounded by Americans made me sound like Tom Hardy.

THE FOOD

This was my least favourite aspect of the country. I was treated to some amazing food in San Francisco/Tiburon and Boston at the start and finish of the leg, but on the road – barring a handful of exceptions – the food was awful.

ALCOHOL

This genuinely annoyed me. All I wanted was to have the occasional beer with my evening food after a long day in the saddle, and I couldn't. I couldn't even joke about it. I would try to order a beer or bend the truth about my age and people would look at me as if they were still in prohibition.

I understand that alcohol abuse is a genuine issue and that

we in the UK are some of the worst for it – especially teenagers. However, I find it ridiculous that you can own a gun but not have a beer. On top of that, half the people at university aren't allowed to drink legally, which just seems wrong. Where is the fun in that?

GUNS

If you agree with the US' firearm policy, there is a strong chance that you are in fact American. I am not going to go into detail on this one, because nothing I say on the matter will benefit anyone – least of all me. I will say that I disagree with the way things are done. I wouldn't mention it if it hadn't made a tangible contribution to my eagerness to leave.

PATRIOTISM

Misguided patriotism to be more specific. I am a big fan of patriotism, and consider myself a patriot in that I love my country. What I dislike is that so many people are wrapped up in the flag and support anything and everything without thinking for themselves. On this note, I would like to say that I don't think the UK gets it entirely right. I think we go the other way and have a tendency to slag off the country (and particularly the government, whichever party happens to be in power) at any opportunity. Perhaps social media makes it seem worse than it is. Granted, sometimes it is very justified, but I believe there needs to be some love for your country. I think a middle ground between the UK and the US attitudes would be ideal.

In the States, once out of the cities, I would say over 90% of houses have some form of American flag hanging outside. Perhaps to them it seems sacrilegious not to, and I can imagine people being chastised for failing to express how great they think the US is. During September 2017, referring to the 'NFL anthem protests', Jason Kander (an American politician) tweeted: *"Patriotism isn't about making everyone stand and salute the flag. Patriotism is about making this a country where everyone wants to* [do that]." It was obviously aimed at a certain president, but I think it illustrates my point quite well. Relating to this, a lot of Americans genuinely seem to think the US is the best at everything. It gets irritating.

When I returned, I had the opportunity to meet the US Ambassador in London. I had been invited to join a group of 'young influential people' (I felt totally out of place), and we were discussing some of the differences between British and American culture. I brought up the fact that patriotism is very prominent across the pond, but I didn't want to offend anyone, and I made a point of not taking a stance on it.* As it turned out, I got the impression most people there felt the same as me, including the ambassador – which surprised me.

TIPS

I found tipping stressful. So much emphasis is put on it and all I wanted was to avoid unintentionally offending someone. It also meant I had to carry round a lot more cash than I was used to. Without a proper wallet, this got on my nerves. Irrational I know.

---

*I know that the whole point of such a debate/discussion is to express your own views, but I felt very much like a fish out of water. Many of the others were budding journalists and perceived 'class leaders'. I was at the opposite end of the spectrum having turned down more than one public-speaking invitation.

I felt it created false, two-faced waiting staff. They were clearly only smiling or flashing that bit of cleavage, to get the extra few bucks (not blaming them). Everything seemed rehearsed and, oddly enough, made them appear far less personable. Surely I'm not alone in thinking that better service depends more on genuine character than false smiles.

POLITICAL CORRECTNESS

Lighten up! Everything seems to be so painfully sanitised.

This links back to the reactions I received when ordering a beer. You remember that kid in school that would remind the teacher about homework? Well, the US is that kid. I felt as though I had to censor every action and sentence to avoid being told off by someone nearby. Sarcasm is completely lost there as well. That's not necessarily a criticism, just an observation that I have a very different sense of humour. In fact, I regularly enjoyed times when people would answer my sarcastic comments with sincerity.

LANGUAGE

They say things incorrectly; and I am not just talking about the pronunciation of things like vitamin and aluminium. I'm referring to the whole *chip/crisp/fry* side of things. On my first evening alone, I was told my burger came with chips. I did not expect my plate to arrive with a load of crisps on it. This may seem very petty, as I suppose they would suggest that the Brits are wrong. But let's put it this way: if America is correct, they would not write '*fish and chips*' on the menu. They do. Every time. I checked.

Rant over. There's an element of truth behind all the above, but obviously I have *slightly* exaggerated some elements for my own amusement. If you are American and you were offended, you are merely backing up a number of the points I raised. Feel free to write a letter of retort highlighting the many British flaws – I would enjoy that greatly. Perhaps copy Chris in on the email as I think he would like it too. These were his words to me:

> *"Now you are off to the good ol' US of A. The land of the free, apparently – so hopefully you won't get shot or arrested."*

AMERICAN SUMMARY

As I progressed around the world, my learning process waned. After Australia, things were still a challenge, but I never doubted my ability to finish. As a result, I found days and experiences becoming more monotonous and I had far less to say about the places I went to. This is something that was reflected in my blog and will be represented in this book.

I could write a day-by-day synopsis for all 42 days of the American leg, but there would be no point. I have already touched on San Francisco, Portland, my wheel problems, the climb over the Rockies and the heat. I don't have much else to add. Navigating Lake Superior offered a few new experiences, so I will elaborate on that part of my journey. Otherwise, a general summary will suffice. For that, I am going to refer to my almost weekly Facebook updates, rather than my blog.

Day 123

I've now done three days riding in the US, and it has become apparent that the coast of California is not actually very sunny. The whole thing is a myth.

Apart from that, most other things are just what you'd expect – a lot of burgers get eaten, not many vegetables get eaten and, by the end of this leg, I think even I will start to fall in love with my accent.

Other things of note: I've passed 20,000 kilometres total, and yesterday I rode through a very big tree...

The tree in question was called the Chandelier Tree. It's 96 metres tall, 6.4 metres in diameter and 2,400 years old. It has a large hole cut in the base to allow cars to drive through. Although very much a tourist attraction, it is something I'm glad I saw. It was one of the few occasions I took a deliberate detour away from my route. The novelty was worth experiencing, and the tree itself truly is enormous. I couldn't fit the whole thing in one camera shot.

Day 132

I'm currently in Idaho, having been through California, Oregon and Washington state.

The coast of Northern California is not warm – so don't bother going there.

Heading inland in Oregon was slightly better, but I somehow managed to crack my rear wheel; so I now have a new one. That's not part of the bike I expected nor wanted to replace, but c'est la vie I guess.

Washington state was good. Heading over the Rockies has brought temperatures to match India and I'm now a tad sunburnt though.

I entered Idaho today, and the big news of the week is that I've reached 13,500 miles – three-quarters of the way round. Big milestone to hit, but honestly it feels like a bit of a piss-take that I still have 4,500 miles to go.

Day 140

I have now done 20 days riding in the US, and, if I'm honest, certain bits of me are starting to hurt. I've just finished crossing Montana, which it turns out is bigger than the UK. There's nothing there though, so I won't be rushing back. I'm now in North Dakota, and as far as I can tell, the other Dakota is better.

Nothing overly interesting has happened this week, so I don't have much else to say. Although it has been hitting mid-forties on the temperature front, so if you live in London, feel free to stop moaning about the so-called heatwave...

Day 146

I hit 15,000 miles today which has put me in a relatively good mood. I 'only' have 3,000 miles to go now, so that means I should be home in about a month. Not gonna lie, after being away for half a year already, that's something I'm really beginning to look forward to. America is starting to take its toll. Turns out it's rather big and the food isn't that great. It's better than India, but I've now had enough mediocre burgers to last a lifetime, and I'm genuinely starting to crave vegetables; not something I ever expected...

Other than today, it's been another boring week. I've just reached the shore of Lake Superior, so I'll be going *round that for quite a while, which no doubt means I'll spend next week being feasted on by mosquitoes.*

Another downside to the States, is the sport. Whilst I'm sure many of you in England are enjoying the likes of Wimbledon, the Ashes, the Tour de France and various other things, I get to watch adverts that are occasionally interrupted by men wearing obscenely large pads, throwing and generally dropping a ball... Or baseball, which is even more boring than cricket.

One other thing, I was in Walmart the other day, and I'm still pondering how anyone can justify buying a two-gallon carton of chocolate milk.

I never gave baseball much of a chance, so perhaps I am being unfair. I no doubt missed the subtle nuances. After all, I am quite happy watching cycling all day, so who am I to comment?

Day 157

I've just stopped in Niagara Falls, so that marks the end of Canada for me. Only five days riding to Boston and quite frankly, I can't wait. I think a couple of days rest will go down nicely.

Canada has been good, but not without difficulties. Over the last nine days I've had three broken spokes, I've encountered some really shite weather, and my knee – which I thought was improving – has decided that life is best spent not moving. (Something that a large proportion of North Americans have also decided.)

In terms of progress, I hit 16,000 miles the other day, so I now have less than 2,000 miles until London.

It feels so close compared to what I've already done, but really, it's still a bit of a trek.

As I mentioned, I'm now at Niagara Falls and to be honest, it's genuinely quite impressive. I'm not normally one to get excited about a load of water falling off a cliff, but it is worth a visit if you're ever nearby. Pictures don't do it justice.

Niagara Falls is stunning. When I arrived on the sunny afternoon of Day 157, the promenade was rammed with thousands of people. With a bike, it was tricky to get a clear view. When I left the next morning at 7am in dull weather, I was the only one there. The spray soaked me when I decided to go as close as the walkway allows. It's quite incredible, and you can really get a sense of the force of the water.

Day 162

I have just cycled across North America (San Francisco to Boston, via Canada):

4497.81 miles
42 days riding
0 rest days
305 hours, 41 minutes in the saddle
4 punctures
1 broken wheel
6 broken spokes
159 hamburgers
8 vegetables
Lots of rather large people...

North America has been a grind, but it feels good to get it done without any days off. I'm now on about 16,755 miles in total and heading into the last stretch.

It hasn't been a great run in terms of mechanical problems, so, thankfully, I have a new wheel waiting for me in Lisbon.

I can't get my head around America just yet. Having ridden every day for the last six weeks, my brain is currently having trouble digesting the fact that I've finished (for a few days anyway).

Despite being here for so long, I still don't understand a lot of what goes on in America – generally regarding food. Something else that baffles me is the amount of people that ask, "Don't you get tired?"

If you are pondering this question yourself, the answer is yes, of course. That's kind of the whole point.

London started to feel within reach after New Zealand, and I don't think two hours went by in America where the finish did not enter my mind. I was doing nothing but follow the same routine for over a month. Every day was different, but very few stood out. When I finished in Boston, I was obviously pleased. However, the fact that I had 'cycled across North America' was the most exciting aspect of it. Without that label, it felt very anticlimactic. The routine had become my life, and I had trouble comprehending not riding.

LAKE SUPERIOR

Between Day 146 and Day 152, I spent my time cycling around Lake Superior. Not all of it obviously; what with it being a lake, that would have left me back where I started and proved extremely counterproductive. Having said that, the premise of my entire trip involved riding in a large circle, so perhaps the whole thing was a complete waste of time.

I skirted the north shore from Duluth to Sault Ste Marie (apparently pronounced "Soo-San-Marie"). The lake itself is unbelievably vast. My blog gives my initial thoughts on the matter:

After 80 miles or so, I reached Duluth, and not long afterwards, Lake Superior – the largest lake in the world! (It's actually not, but I'm excluding the Caspian Sea because it's saline, and saying I'm on the shore of the second largest lake doesn't have the same ring to it.)

I'm curious, can I call the edge of a lake the coast? Or is 'shore' the only suitable word? To be honest, it's difficult to see it as a lake when looking out towards it. It is so big, and I'm going to be following the edge of it for a fair while.

I'm reminded of a time when standing on the edge of Lake Geneva (Lac Léman for any French people), and a mate of mine turned to me and said, "Is that bit over there the sea?" If you're reading this, you know who you are, and that remains the stupidest thing you have ever said, not least because Switzerland is a land-locked country. Regardless, if you had said that whilst on the edge of Lake Superior, it would have been more excusable - it really is bloody massive. [Edit: he's actually said far worse, but I left that in for dramatic effect]

My second day on Lake Superior ended in a town called Grand Marais, which was my favourite stop for the whole of America. The weather certainly helped, but, considering I stayed in a tent that night, I think the two balance each other out. It's a picturesque lakeside town, and it felt like the perfect place to chill out.

I was never comfortable in the US. I always felt a little tense, as though I could easily step out of line and say something that would offend at least one person within earshot. I can't put my finger on exactly what it was, but I viewed it as the opposite end of the spectrum to Australia, with England somewhere in the middle. I will try to elaborate.

I have grown up with England as my norm. There is an element of political correctness in the air, but the tone is always brought back down by the constant use of sarcastic humour. Australia lived up to its stereotype. People spend all day in flip flops on the beach, everything is very laissez-faire, and 'c*nt' is a term of endearment rather than an insult (genuinely).

In America, I felt that if you called the wrong person that word, you would get a bullet in the head. Perhaps it was the increased drinking age that made me subconsciously think everything was stricter, or perhaps it was again my stereotypical ideas and I am being unfair. On my second day of riding in California, I was coming into the final 30 kilometres when I saw that a car had veered off the side of the road and into a ditch. I had seen much worse in India, but, as I drew alongside and looked back, I saw bullet holes in the windscreen. That shocked me. I had never been exposed to anything like that before and I spent the remainder of the day on edge.

As I said, I am open to the idea that my depiction of the country is skewed, but Grand Marais was the only place I felt I could actually relax. Even in San Francisco and Boston I was worried I would say something considered rude. I felt relaxed enough in Grand Marais to have another go at ordering a beer; although, as usual, it ended in failure.

The next day, I crossed over into Canada and was finally allowed to have that beer I had been craving. I liked Canada, but Thunder Bay – where I stayed that night – was a stark contrast to the town I had enjoyed the evening before. I was pulled over by the police on the way in as well, which was a first for me. Not for anything exciting mind, only to tell me that I couldn't cycle on the road I was on.

Day 4 on Lake Superior (Day 149 in total) was marred by knee pain, but largely uneventful. Day 5 was wet, really wet. Imagine a tropical rainstorm and decrease the temperature by 30°C. Then imagine having to cycle for over eight hours in it, and sleep in a tent at the end. Yeah, that's how I felt. I was miserable and cold the whole day, and was made even more miserable by the prospect of camping:

Waking up to the sound of rain set the tone for the day this morning. Long story short – I got wet, I had a headwind, and the idea of camping in this weather was making me as gloomy as possible.

Mentally, it was one of the hardest mornings I've had, and, honestly, this was the first time that I've wanted nothing more than for the trip to be over.

After stopping for some food at Marathon, the rain got worse. The wind got better though, so my feelings stayed roughly the same. It's also worth mentioning that today was far from flat, and, unlike yesterday, I did not enjoy heading uphill. My knee started hurting again to add to my woes. Same knee, but in a different place, so I don't know why that is.

I'm feeling a bit better now, so I may have played down the day's ride, but I hit a low point today. To add insult to injury, a spoke broke with two kilometres to go. I had actually been expecting it all day. It's been six days since it last happened, and based on current form, I was due another. To be fair, it's a good thing it broke so late, as I was able to 'limp' the final few minutes and sort it out once I'd finished.

Thankfully, where I am now has remained fairly dry, so I didn't have to put up a tent in the rain, which is something I was dreading. Although, I've set up camp on the decking outside the 'tourist office', which is covered anyway.

I owe a big thanks to Alex, who I've spent a fair bit of the evening with. It's been good to have a normal conversation with someone, rather than just spend the evening in a state of self-pity.

I've also found a dryer, which means I don't have to put on wet clothes in the morning, so I'm feeling slightly better about life... Although my shoes will still be wet.

Where I'm staying now (White River), has a lot of references to Winnie the Pooh. Can somebody please tell me the significance?

Only other thing to mention is that, as I'm writing this, a mosquito has landed on my nose, and I've just gone and hit myself straight in the face.

To answer my own question for anyone else wondering: A.A. Milne's inspiration for the stories was a bear in London Zoo called Winnie. The bear in question was originally found in White River, before being taken to England. Hence the references that are dotted around the place. Before anyone jumps to any conclusions and thinks it might be worth a visit. It's not. Take my word for it.

Alex was a guy who came over to speak to me whilst I was fixing my spoke. He was working with a group of truckers, and, being in his mid-twenties, he was half the age of any of his colleagues. With a tough day fresh in my mind and the tedious task of fixing a wheel at hand, I wasn't in the best mood when he started talking to me. It's funny how something as simple as a normal conversation can completely change your mood.

After he had left me to finish getting sorted (put up the tent and shower in a petrol station), we went to grab dinner together. It seemed to be the only restaurant in town, and the food was well below par. Regardless, the company was a pleasant and an unexpected distraction. I owe him thanks for keeping my spirits up when I otherwise would have remained miserable all evening.

That is not the only time I had dinner or spent an evening with a new acquaintance. I didn't buy into the whole 'bicycle touring' ethos about going out and finding strangers to talk to every night. I'm good at being on my own, and I got myself in a zone where I blocked out a lot. That is not to say I would turn down company if others approached or invited me to join. It would always add some interest to my evening, even when the company was not so desirable.

Take Goa for instance. I was eating at a restaurant, and there were two other people there, one of whom was a middle-aged Englishman who spent most of his time talking about how wonderful he was. I don't know whether he was talking to me or whether he spent every evening saying the same stuff, regardless of who or what was within earshot. He was harmless and very easy to laugh at, so I didn't find the whole thing too annoying. He talked in depth about how most people don't really travel and don't experience the real side to the country. I found this ironic since we were sitting in Goa, one of the only places in India where I didn't see myself as a novelty.

Conversely, my evening in Clare – the night before riding into Adelaide – was brilliant, and I experienced incredible levels of generosity and hospitality. I was coming to the end of a nine-and-a-half-hour day, when a woman named Helen pulled over in front of me and waved me down. She had heard about some idiot cycling around the world on the radio that morning (presumably my interview), and she stopped me on the off chance that it was me. She then – without any hesitation – invited me for dinner and offered me a bed for the night. There was nothing forced about the offer, she just happened to be one of the kindest people I came across. I had already booked a place to stay for the night, so I declined the bed, but said I would ride round to her house for dinner.

When I arrived, not only had she prepared a bloody good meal, but it also turned out to be her birthday, and they were having a small family get-together. I felt I was intruding a bit, but the four of them could not have made me feel more welcome. Her son was an ex-professional cyclist, which was also very cool.

People were great to me in Australia. In Wollongong, two women invited me over to their table to eat with them. It was the day before a big sports competition (the CrossFit Pacific Regionals), and they had assumed I was also there to watch it. I think they took pity on me eating by myself.

Going back to Lake Superior and White River, I started early the next morning, largely because I received a rude awakening from the weather. When I had consulted some more practised campers back in Australia, they reassured me that condensation was completely normal, and that there was not much I could do about it. Whether that is true or not, it seemed rather idiotic. The only reason I bothered with the tent was to keep the potential wet weather out, yet there I was getting soggy anyway. I may as well have slept under a dodgy tap.

My solution was to leave the outer tent flap wide open. This worked perfectly on the other occasions I tried it, when the weather remained dry. It wasn't always warm, but I had a suitable sleeping bag, so I managed. However, the wet weather in White River highlighted a large flaw in my strategy:

Much like yesterday, I was woken up to rain this morning. However, rather than waking up to the sound of rain, I was woken up by the rain... at 3am.

Despite pitching my tent under a roof, I still got hit very hard by the storm that arrived. The wind was the major problem, and, after 10 minutes of holding my tent steady from the inside, I decided to go outside and move it to a more sheltered spot. This was easier said than done, given that I had tied the tent to a table (obviously I couldn't peg it into the decking). It would have looked a bit odd to any passers-by: a teenager with ridiculous tan lines, trying to carry a tent 10 feet, only wearing boxers, in the driving rain, at three o'clock in the morning. But anyway, I managed it, and it solved the problem. I didn't get much sleep though.

That was the last time I used my tent. The ensuing day passed surprisingly well. I was already sleep deprived, so that was nothing out of the ordinary, and, by the time I set off, the storm had moved on. It ended up being a straightforward and enjoyable day in the saddle.

Day 152 was set to be my last skirting the edge of Lake Superior. I was heading for Sault Ste Marie and would reach it after 120 kilometres. I would then continue west, away from the lake. I felt a bit shit when I set off in the morning. There was no particular reason for it; the weather was good and the wind was fine, but my legs felt sluggish and I couldn't get comfortable on the bike. By this point in the trip, I never planned to stop as early as 45 kilometres, but, because of how I was feeling, I decided it would be a good idea.

When I stopped, I met a group of six or seven other people who were cycling across Canada. They had all set off on their own or in a pair, but had crossed paths along the way and were now cycling together as a group. I rode the rest of the way with them to Sault Ste Marie, where they all stopped for the evening. That 75-kilometre stretch was one of my better ones. Throughout my North American stint, I had become even more focused on just getting the job done. All I could think of for six weeks was finishing in Boston. I built up a steely determination that got me through the really shit days. Conversely, I found it very difficult to switch off and enjoy myself when things actually went my way.

When I first pulled into where I was stopping and saw the other bikes laden with panniers, I nearly turned around and carried on cycling. I knew I would get caught up with them. This was the mindset I found myself in; it did not occur to me that it could be a good thing. I have no regrets about that. I understand if some of you read this and think I was nothing more than a miserable bastard. The truth is, if I had not ridden with that attitude, some of the things I went through would have broken me.

A similar thing was going through my head in India on Day 43, when I rejected the offer of tea. I'm very happy I made the opposite decision on Day 152 and joined up with that group of cyclists. I managed to relax a bit whilst riding with the others. It was there I saw the appeal of a leisurely ride around a country (or a planet): no stress of a daily target, riding with your mates as far or for as little as you want and having a few beers in the evening. Not a bad way to spend a couple of weeks; it just wasn't what I had set out to do. So, despite them trying to convince me to set up camp for the evening with them, I carried on for my final 70-kilometre stretch.

It was originally shaping up to be an extremely tedious day, but having some company for part of it resulted in it being a really good one. Even the final stretch on my own was enjoyable. After turning away from Lake Superior for the final time, the rest of the day passed by with ease.

A MASSIVE
THANK YOU

Boston marked the final time that I was put up by others. When I landed in Lisbon, I stayed in a hotel with Mum and Anna, and my next stop after that was London. I therefore feel this a fitting place to say thank you to all those who were kind enough to look after me, even if it was just for an evening.

JANE, JOHNNY AND BARNABY

They hosted me, my parents and my sister, as well as some other friends, on my first evening of the trip. I was able to shower and eat before boarding the overnight ferry, and it was fantastic for calming my nerves.

FERESHTE, MOSIN AND BOB

When I was in Mumbai, I stayed with Fereshte. I have talked about my time there already, but she deserves another mention. Fereshte was no more than a contact of a friend, yet she gave me somewhere to stay, fed me and prepared me for the forthcoming part of my ride. She also organised for my bike box to be sent across India by train to Kolkata once I had left Mumbai. Mosin was the one who showed me round the city during the day. He did a wonderful job of introducing me to many of the subtleties of Indian culture. Not only that, but he made my time there extremely enjoyable. There were very few people in India that I was able to relate to as well as him.

I was introduced to Bob by Fereshte during my final evening in Mumbai. He took it upon himself to ensure I remained safe. Had I needed it, he would have been on hand to provide any assistance he could.

DEBASHIS AND RAJAT

Debashis was another contact of a friend, and, like Fereshte in Mumbai, helped to sort many of the logistics in Kolkata with the help of Rajat, who worked in his team. Unfortunately, despite all his help, Dad and I never actually got to meet Debashis. He had an important family commitment on the days that we were in Kolkata, but Rajat took great pains to help us throughout our time. Rajat continued to offer support throughout the rest of my trip, which was always greatly appreciated.

RICHARD AND SARA BROWN

Mum and I stayed with them during our time in Singapore. They went above and beyond normal hospitality, and completely put their own lives on hold to work around our visit and needs. Our time there was wonderful and completely stress-free.

THE ROONEY FAMILY

I loved Perth, and a lot of that was due to the Rooney family (Damian, Lily and their four kids). They welcomed me like a close friend, and made me feel comfortable from the outset. I arrived to a barbeque at the house of a friend of theirs (typically Australian), and things only got better. I particularly enjoyed playing some Aussie rules with Jack and George. My favourite part was the lead-out I received from the whole family. Damian joined me for the first 90 kilometres when I rode out of Perth, but all of them joined me for the first mile. It was a brilliant farewell.

JEN

She bought me breakfast when I rode through Albany. That was also the last extended conversation I had with anyone for a while.

HELEN, WILL, OLIVIA AND JOHN

I have recently mentioned my evening in Clare, Australia, but I want to reiterate the unparalleled generosity that I was shown by Helen and her family.

THE VAILE FAMILY

Adelaide was also wonderful, and was where I stayed with the Vailes. I must have completely ruined their plans when I changed schedule four days before arriving, asking to stay an extra night. As ever, I received an amazing welcome. Julian organised a necessary physio session and bike service for my day off. He then convinced a group of his friends to ride out of Adelaide with me; something that remains a highlight. They also cooked me a roast dinner on the second evening. I had been craving one for weeks, and it went down a treat.

THE ELSWORTHY FAMILY

I have mentioned my days with them already, but I thoroughly enjoyed every second I spent with Ray, Richard, Steve, Leanne and Sam. Steve also organised and paid for my bike box to be transported from Perth to Brisbane.

JON, SUZIE AND JACK ADAMS

Having driven out very early to join me some 40 miles outside Sydney, Jon and Jack accompanied me into the city on their mountain bikes, and then invited me, my cousin Steph and Doug up to their apartment overlooking Bondi beach for a drink.

STRAVA FRIENDS

A guy called Damien also joined me for much of the day from Wollongong to Sydney, along with Jon and Jack Adams. I had bumped into him the evening before on his commute home and he showed me a route out of the city the next morning. Giles and Paddy did a similar thing in Wellington, after getting in touch through Strava; as did Steve on Day 142 in North Dakota, Peter in Brisbane and Paul in the UK. Many thanks to you all!

STEPH AND DOUG

I couldn't have asked for anything better for my day in Sydney. Spending it with my cousin was wonderfully surreal. Of the whole trip, this was the day that felt most like a holiday.

THE O'SULLIVAN FAMILY

Dom, Sarah and their boys looked after me during my brief stop in Brisbane. This was no mean feat. Dom rode into the city with me that morning, but had also organised a physio session, a full bike service and helped me pack my bike up – all in one afternoon. They had housed my bike box for a couple of weeks too. I flew out the next morning, and it's a shame I didn't get to spend more time with them in Brisbane.

NIGEL AND SONIA

Friends of a friend, they cooked for me and Dad when we stopped for the evening in New Plymouth, New Zealand. It was delicious, thank you.

ALISON DAVIS AND FAMILY

They gave me a stunning introduction to California and an amazing place to stay whilst in San Francisco. I was also treated to possibly my favourite meal of the whole American leg. Alison also organised and paid for transport across North America for my bike box, which was the third trip it had to make on its own.

SHOWERS PASS, FRASER AND KYLE RANSON AND TIM

My brief stop in Portland was extremely eventful. I owe many thanks to Showers Pass as a company for their contribution to my whole trip. Fraser was responsible for supplying me with much of my kit back in the UK and for helping keep my spirits up with his regular contributions to my blog. Kyle saved my bike and gave me breakfast whilst I was in Portland. Tim joined me for the ride as I left Portland and provided some brilliant company. He stayed with me for so long that I think he would have ridden further than I did by the time he got home again.

JIM AND SUE BERNBECK

They took me in for the evening I was in Canandaigua (after Niagara Falls). They gave me a superb meal and a bed for the night. It had been over a month since I had spent that long with people, and it was a fantastic reintroduction to normal human behaviour.

THE HAILS (DAVID, KELLY, ALEX AND RORY)

They packed up their holiday in double quick time in order to get back to meet me in Boston. They invited me to the hotel where they were spending the night, let me use their shower and bought me lunch. I'm not sure what they got out of the deal!

THE STEEL FAMILY

Last, but definitely not least, is the Steel family in Boston (Liz, Chris, Alex and Georgina). Friends of friends, they housed my bike box for weeks, put me up, arranged a press interview for me, cooked me a fabulous meal and gave me a lift to the airport. I had a great time there. After 42 days' consecutive riding, I eventually managed to switch off completely, which is something I often failed to do. This made Lisbon a bit stressful, but my time with the Steels was wonderful. On the way to the airport with Alex, I realised that, amongst other things, I had missed out on six months' worth of music. There was nothing overly groundbreaking from recollection, but it was a fact that made my detachment feel more substantial than I had initially appreciated.

I cannot possibly do justice to how grateful I am to all these people. They all went out of their way to help and to look after me, often having to accommodate my last-minute needs. Every one of them had a huge impact on my trip, and therefore a significant impact on me.

Thank you!

CRASH

Throughout the whole trip, I only fell off once. It was fairly painful, very annoying and extremely embarrassing. It happened on Day 168 whilst riding through San Sebastián (beautiful place, worth a visit). By this point in my trip, it was deep into the Spanish summer, and I had just been joined by Dad and Henry. The sun was out, and I was coming to the end of what had so far been a successful journey. All in all, I was feeling good about life.

I'd had a tedious week riding up through Portugal and Spain, but reaching the northern coast had brought some stunning scenery and, more importantly, some company. I had rediscovered my love of cycling the evening before, and was managing to genuinely enjoy myself for the first time in a long while.

The ride up through the Iberian Peninsula was surprisingly difficult. When I relaxed at the end of America, I fell into a state of complacency. Lisbon became a desperate rush to get myself prepared for the last stage of my ride, and, once on my bike, I found the task at hand much harder than expected.

I approached the final leg without any focus, assuming that I would knock off the remaining miles with ease. However, my complacency meant I neglected my body. I didn't eat or drink enough to overcome the scorching temperatures, and I hadn't appreciated the effect a few rest days would have on my body. Whilst my legs were relatively fresh, the numerous other aches around my body made themselves known. The bruises on my hands became extremely noticeable, and my arse was constantly uncomfortable. I had five days' riding from Lisbon to where I would meet Dad and Henry. With that target so close, I thought I would manage, no matter what state my head was in. I was wrong – I struggled.

During that period, most of the countryside I travelled through was dry and arid. Some of the towns and cities were pretty, but excitement was hard to come by in-between. My daily mileage increased a bit over the final leg, and I was uncharacteristically laboured to begin with. The hours dragged on, the heat became an obstacle and I found it challenging to block out thoughts of the imminent finish. I was psyching myself out, and everything became a chore.

Four days after leaving Lisbon, I managed to get my act together again. I suppressed the lethargy that I had left Boston with and regained my mental focus. The difficulties were all in my head, and, after concentrating, I became comfortable again.

By the time I met Dad and Henry in Zumaia, I was back in control. I once again managed to push the aches and pains to the back of my mind, and I strolled through 100 miles with ease. The day leading up to my arrival in Zumaia helped. Once north of Vitoria, Spain evolved into a different country. The boring plains were replaced by lush hills. The roads became smooth, and my legs came alive. I reached the Bay of Biscay on a significant high.

The others arrived in Zumaia an hour or two after me, to end my solitude for the final time. Had they met me 48 hours earlier I would have broken down with relief. I lacked all composure throughout the middle portion of Spain, and was praying for some respite. As it happened, by regaining control over my mental state, I was just pleased for the company, rather than dependent upon it.

The following day, however, my confidence was once again pegged back a notch. The overall ride was good, but the day was marred by a sharp introduction to the tarmac. The surroundings were stunning, and the scenery continued to impress. Henry and I were riding through San Sebastián when we passed the cathedral. He suggested that we turn around and have another look. I had spent the last six months avoiding culture as much as possible, but, on this occasion, I agreed. I slowed down, attempted to mount the kerb and failed. It wasn't even a regular section of kerb; it was at a set of traffic lights, so it was – at most – an inch high. I got the angle wrong, lost my front wheel and very unceremoniously hit the deck. I landed on my head so, fortunately, my bike was unharmed. I did, however, crack my helmet and had to borrow my dad's for the remainder of the trip (he was driving the car at this point).

I was irrationally upset about switching helmets. I'd ridden so far in mine that it felt like a betrayal to finish the trip in a different one. I'm not usually a sentimental person, but I still have the cracked one at home. It holds the same value as the T-shirt I wore for the first two weeks in India. Dad had a spare helmet brought out the next day when Nige (my godfather) joined us. Thankfully, this meant that Dad didn't completely miss out on the cycling, but he did refuse to take his original helmet back on the grounds that I had spent 40 hours sweating in it.

With reference to the crash, and as far as significant injuries go, I was unhurt. I jarred my wrist and shoulder, but it was my ego that took the brunt. I had ridden over 17,000 miles, through

21 countries – including India. I had survived numerous near misses, only to come unstuck under very embarrassing circumstances in a crowded town centre. If you were there, thank you for not laughing.

HELMET

I wore a helmet the whole way round the world. Some people disagree with the need to wear one, a view that I think is silly. I only fell off my bike once, and I consider myself lucky in that regard. Even so, had I not been wearing a helmet, I very much doubt I would have finished the trip on time, if at all. It only takes one careless moment or one stupid driver, so what are the reasons for not wearing one?

If you find your helmet uncomfortable, buy one that fits. If you find it too hot, buy one with more ventilation. If you find it ugly, trust me when I say that you look more of an idiot when not wearing it. Helmet development has come on enough over the years for none of these to be a legitimate excuse.

I know of, and have seen, many people who take their helmet off and clip it somewhere on their bike when cycle touring. This makes no sense to me. You're still carrying the sodding thing, so just stick it on your bonce! Not only that, but if it's performance you are after, the aerodynamics of a helmet are designed with the assumption that it will be worn on your head.

There are, however, a few scenarios where you can be forgiven for not wearing one. Firstly, a five-minute cycle to the shops. Whilst logic dictates that you should still wear one on such a trip, I appreciate that I would be fighting a losing battle in this instance.

Secondly, traditional British hill-climb races. If you find yourself doing one, you may be willing to risk death in order to save the couple of seconds that leaving your helmet at the bottom will provide. That is completely understandable. No one wants to lose.

At the end of the day, if you've got a helmet, you might as well wear it. Personally, I think the decision is simple: any positives you can find in leaving your helmet at home are drastically outweighed by the prospect of a traumatic brain injury.

NAIVELY AMBITIOUS

Naivety is a wonderful thing. It is present in all areas of life, and I've even read a few things about how naivety has benefitted people and organisations in the business world. For now, I'll stick to my experiences. My plan to cycle around the world was the epitome of being naively ambitious. Sure, I did a lot of research and planning before I set off, but the moment I came up with the idea at the tender age of 17 was the moment I decided I was going to do it. When I started researching, discovering it was achievable was a fortunate coincidence, because I would have given it a go anyway. The fact that no one my age had ever done it didn't bother me. I believed I was capable, and I didn't dwell on the consequences. That would only have held me back.

I wasn't the first, I wasn't the fastest and I'm sure I won't be the youngest for long. Seven years before I set off, Mark Beaumont broke the speed record by riding 100 miles a day. The same daily distance as my attempt. In 2017, he broke the record again, this time riding 240 miles a day. On his first attempt, he smashed the then record and paved the way for other challengers to come. In terms of racing, that original pace would now be considered 'pedestrian'. At the time, it was extremely fast. It just goes to show how perceptions change.

I wasn't racing, but I set myself what I considered to be a respectable target. My age will not be extraordinary for long. To an extent, being the first is very experimental. Once someone has gone before you, it's easier to copy them and rectify the mistakes they made. I hope I have helped start the ball rolling for younger people. I don't care whether my unofficial title is taken off me. I hope that, to some extent, I have shown what's possible and that I have inspired a younger generation to push not only their own but human limits.

Fast-forward to September the following year – the beginning of my second year at Loughborough University and when I was about to turn 21 – I was pondering the idea of doing a marathon. I used to run a bit when I was in school, but I stopped when I started getting shin splints. Since then, I hadn't really done much running at all. Regardless, I was confident that I would be able to complete a marathon.

Marathons have a formidable reputation. People build them up in their head to such an extent that they become afraid of the concept. Indeed, they are a very difficult thing to do, but I never for one minute looked at it like this. I just told myself it was three to four hours of exercise. Give me a bike, and I'll pedal for days; I never considered that I wouldn't be able to run for a few hours.

Along the same lines of not over-thinking it, I didn't want to make a big thing of it. I wasn't going to enter an official event, instead I decided I would just go for a 26.2-mile run and record it on my phone.

I did a couple of five or six kilometre runs in early October. That allowed me to get an idea of the pace I could do. I then put the running on hold for a short while as I was still training for the tail end of the cycling season. I therefore decided to target it in November.

My theory was this: aerobically, I was easily capable of running for that length of time. I just needed to do a bit of training to get my legs accustomed to the movement of running, rather than cycling. This is not far from being complete and utter nonsense, but naivety reigned supreme, and I convinced myself that it was fact.

I started my training on 1st November. I told myself that, by the end of the month, I would run a marathon in under three and a half hours. I had to give myself a challenging time, otherwise I felt I had no excuse not to go out and do it straight away.

So, on the 1st (a Tuesday), I ran 10 kilometres. By the Sunday, I was up to 13 kilometres, but running a bit faster (a marathon is 42.2 kilometres). I didn't have the timescale to allow myself a proper amount of rest, so I just continued to increase the intensity. After 10 days of running, the longest I had done was 13.6 kilometres, but I again threw caution to the wind and decided to reduce my target marathon time. I set my sights on a time of three hours, as that's the pace I was hovering around.

I drove back to London for the first weekend. I went for a four-hour ride on the Saturday (purely for enjoyment), then went to the pub with some mates in the evening. I normally don't drink when I have a big event on the horizon, but I figured the goal was still over three weeks away, so a few beers wouldn't pose a problem. On the Sunday, we went out for a family lunch, and I ate a lot of food, none of which would have benefitted my performance. So, I essentially had the weekend off.

I talked over my idea with a few people that weekend. Most seemed to think both my theory and I were idiotic. In fact, people were far more incredulous about my marathon plans than when I had said I would cycle around the world. Weird.

On the second Friday (11 days into my 30-day target), I ran my first half-marathon. Over the previous week or so, I had come up with a 10-kilometre loop and an 11-kilometre loop. I did them both once, and finished in 1:25:30.

I went for a short, but hideously wet, ride on the Saturday, but did nothing else in terms of training that weekend. Again, not ideal preparation. Nevertheless, on the Monday (14th November) I changed my mind again. I was sitting in a lecture, bored out of my mind and I thought, *Sod it. I'm bored of running, let's do it tonight.*

I went to the shops, bought some Powerade and convinced myself it was a good idea. I was going to do the same loops I had done in my half-marathon a couple of days earlier, but do them both twice. Each loop finished back at my house. I don't like running with a bottle, so I left three Powerade bottles outside the entrance – each less than half full – so I would be able to grab one each time I came past. I'd drink the contents and chuck the bottle in a bin 500 metres down the road.

These loops also helped me mentally. It broke the effort up into quarters, so I could easily gauge my pace and how much I was hurting. From my brief training, I knew I could sustain a sub-three-hour pace for half a marathon. Based on how I felt during that effort, I thought I should be able to hold that speed for at least 30 kilometres. So, I just kept telling myself to get to that point and then hang on for the final 45 minutes.

The last hour really hurt. It's the most painful situation I have been in that did not involve a bike, but I finished my marathon in 2:56:46. I ran a further 200 metres just to make certain I had done the distance, then I stopped. My routes hadn't worked out exactly, so when I finished I was actually 500 metres away from my house. It took me over 10 minutes to get home. As soon as I stopped running, my legs stopped working and I could hardly walk. My feet were completely ruined as well. Seven months on, I still had two dead toenails.

I started out with a plan to run a 3:30:00 marathon with four weeks' training. I ran sub-three hours with only two weeks' training, and I only decided when I was going to do it four hours before the attempt. I didn't think anything through, didn't overcomplicate anything and, although most people thought I was stupid, I exceeded even my own expectations.

These same principles applied to my cycle around the world, but it's not so easy for most people to relate to, and I find it harder to get my point across. Your body can be pushed much harder than you think. Whatever you are doing, always aim to be naively ambitious. Do not go jumping off a building expecting to fly, but add an extra 10 minutes to your run, or another five kilometres to your cycle. Unless you feel like you are literally about to die, your body will be capable. Don't just accept the norms of what others have put in place: decide for yourself.

I mentioned how people were more doubtful of my marathon challenge than my round-the-world plans. This seems a bit odd, but it's true. I think it comes down to the fact that people struggle to relate to what cycling around the world involves, whereas a marathon is something lots of people do and lots of people know to be difficult. In the same vein, people at university were more surprised by my run than my cycle.

To put it into context, that marathon took me less than three hours. On a daily basis of cycling around the world, I was cycling for an average of seven hours. Sometimes more intense, sometimes less. Had I trained as much for running as I did for cycling, I would equate running a marathon to two-thirds the difficulty of cycling 100 miles on a fully laden bike. Obviously, it's not quite that simple to quantify, but bear with the analogy.

Then, if you factor in that I am finding my own food, not sleeping in my own bed, dealing with adverse weather, navigating through alien countries and cultures, and repeating it every day for six long months, it puts a different spin on it.

The length of the challenge alone is the hardest part to deal with, so, to be honest, it's not remotely comparable to a one-off event. I don't want to sound arrogant, but I was asked on more than one occasion if what I did was difficult. I hope this provides some context.

As for my limits, I didn't find them. I pushed harder than I ever thought I would have to, but I dealt with it better than expected. Until you find your breaking point, it's impossible to know where it is. I came up with the idea at the age of 17. If I had set off then and there, would I have managed? Who knows. It's definitely possible, but it's going to fall to someone else to prove it.

FRANCE:
SECOND TIME LUCKY

I love France. I have been fortunate enough to spend a lot of time there; specifically, in the Alps. I love the food, I love the mountains and, unlike a lot of Brits, I quite like the people too. However, I experienced a new side to the country when I rode through it in January – one that I was not so fond of. Returning to France at the back end of my trip occurred just after my little crash, and I seemed destined to continue where I had left off. Thankfully, my fortunes were due to change.

The final five days up through France (Days 168–172), were the best consecutive five days of my trip. Nige joined us on Day 169 to make it a group of four. This meant, with one of them driving the car – I had two people riding with me. The rides flew by. I can't speak for the others, but, by this point, 100 miles was a short day in the saddle for me. My legs handled the distance with ease, and being amongst friends meant the mental side posed no issues either.

Riding with others highlighted how my body had changed. When I set off in January, I didn't think my legs would get that much stronger. I thought the sheer volume and lack of rest would leave me too fatigued to notice any improvements. Happily, that was not the case. I didn't see the same gains that I would have done had I been on a structured training plan, but I was a far better cyclist than six months earlier.

It wasn't only my legs and head that had matured, but my resistance to adverse weather also became apparent. Temperatures above 30°C on Day 170 saw both Henry and Dad suffer. It was here that I realised how much of an effect the temperatures I endured in the US had had on me. I felt fine. Obviously, it was warmer than I would have liked, but I didn't need to recover in the shade and I didn't have a desperate need to replenish my water supply. Even two years on, I find myself needing far less water than most people on a ride. That is not a bragging point, it's just an observation.

The only real hiccup during this stint came on Day 171, when our car broke down for a couple of hours. However, even that sorted itself out eventually.

At the end of Day 171, I wrote the following:

After almost seven months, this is my last full night abroad. I haven't quite got my head around that; maybe it's because I still have to cycle 100 miles tomorrow, and maybe something will sink in when I get on the ferry. For now, I'm still on the road. Quite frankly, I feel like I have finally got used to it! Better late than never I suppose.

The last week has been brilliant with the company I have had, but I still can't wait to get home. Whilst it has been easier, the pressure (much of which is self-inflicted) and the stress are still there. I don't think I have felt completely relaxed for almost a year.

In many ways, you would think that the freedom one has when 'cycling around the world' eliminates these problems. But, unless you are taking years to do it and don't mind taking a week off every three days (i.e. you don't have a set time frame), then I think stress is unavoidable. At least it has been for me... And I think that is what I'm looking forward to getting rid of the most.

Those five days felt almost like a holiday, but, no matter how hard I tried, I couldn't shake the weight off my shoulders. I wanted to relax, but the closer I was to the finish, the more I felt the pressure building. I think, above all, I was impatient. I just wanted it to be over. I didn't want to stop in the evenings. I knew by then that I was capable of stretching myself over those last few days, and I have no doubt that I could have doubled the mileage had I needed to. I enjoyed my time in France with Dad, Henry and Nige immensely, but there was an underlying stress I could not dislodge. It was frustrating. The final 1,000 miles of my trip felt like an unnecessary formality. I had already proved to myself that I was capable, and I knew that nothing would break me. Of course, I struggled at points after Lisbon, but I was never close to being derailed. I was learning nothing new and had already been through the toughest moments.

When we arrived at the ferry in Cherbourg, on Day 172, I had to work hard to keep my emotions in check. Blocking out thoughts of the finish was even more difficult than usual. I had effectively completed my very big circle, but I told myself I needed to maintain my composure until I turned into my road, two days later.

DAY 174

The final day from Winchester to London was a truly surreal experience for me. I honestly don't know what emotion I was feeling. Whatever it was, it had been building since Lisbon two weeks earlier. The final 48 hours of the ride all had a similar feel.

When I reached the ferry in Cherbourg at the end of Day 172, I came to some realisation of how close I was. I had finished mainland Europe and only had two short days in England to go.

I was met in Poole – the other side of the crossing – by friends congratulating me, along with Mum and Anna. I obviously appreciated it, but I hadn't finished yet and I was genuinely taken aback at first. I remained overly focused on what I had left to do (deliberately so), and it felt a bit strange hearing people tell me how well I had done. I was also still feeling restless and a large part of me wanted to ride the 120 miles to London that night. A week earlier we had decided to aim for a specific finish date, and plans had been made for that day since then, so I had to be patient.

The penultimate day was only 50 miles, and, after having a leisurely breakfast, we rolled out as a group of eight. As they had done on my first day of the trip, many of the Strictly CC guys

joined me for one or both of my final two days. I owe all of them
a thank you; not just for that, but for taking me out on rides ever
since I started cycling.

After what felt like a very short day, we arrived in Winchester,
and I was able to chill out ahead of my final day. I wrote a one-line
blog post and went for a very good meal with Dad, Henry, Chris
and Sara. Despite the distractions, I stubbornly maintained my
focus. I was terrified of finishing. Over the last week, I had done
nothing but concentrate on the day-to-day cycle. I was worried I
would get ahead of myself. The evening in Winchester offered a
different scenario. Focusing on the following day meant focusing
on the finish. I started to feel genuine nerves, akin to when I had
left England six months earlier.

I felt a significant amount of pressure on me during that
final ride. I had time constraints, which only added to my usual
self-inflicted stress. Over the previous few days, to my surprise,
I'd had a few TV and radio stations telling me they were going
to show up at my finish line, but this meant I needed to arrive
within a certain time frame. Mum was at home coordinating
the whole thing with the reporting stations, friends, family and
neighbours.

I reached the magic number of 18,000 miles when I was 46
miles from home, and that in itself was a big relief. I had known
I wouldn't fall short, but it was still nice to have it verified by the
number ticking over on my Garmin.

Coming into London, via Hampton Court, was where my
head stopped making sense of things. I suddenly found myself
on a route I had ridden loads of times. I stopped relying on my
Garmin for the first time in months and went into autopilot. I
don't remember much of the last few miles; it was all a blur.

As I rounded the final few corners, everyone riding with me
eased off and let me ride in alone. As I turned into my road, I

was suddenly faced with hundreds of people. I was blown away by the reception and didn't really know what to do. I threw a little victory salute as I rode under a banner that stretched across our road and then put the brakes on for the final time.

From the second I put my foot down, I was fighting back tears. I was standing on my own, overwhelmed and confused. Mum came over to me, and that's when I started crying. I felt a massive wave of relief. There's no point hiding it, my friends happily remind me of the fact I started crying at every opportunity. The cameras only made the whole thing more public. They wanted me standing on my own, and I felt a bit silly and self-conscious doing so.

Within a few minutes of finishing, I had given three interviews on camera. The first of which, I don't think made much sense. I couldn't stop the tears, let alone speak. It took me a long time to compose myself.

It was all a bit of a whirlwind. After speaking to lots of people, eating some food and taking some pictures, I went inside to shower. Once back in my own house, it felt as if I had never been away. Everything was so familiar that I couldn't help but laugh when walking into my bedroom. It was over.

It took me a very long time to make sense of everything that happened. In the days that followed, I had two television interviews, one of which involved getting a train up to Manchester the day after finishing. It was a great experience and a great honour to be on the *BBC Breakfast* couch, but it meant that I didn't get much time to relax.

A week later, I was back on my bike and testing myself on some Alpine climbs. I didn't stop. I just got on with the next stage of my life. I realised early on that nothing was going to wait for me to catch my breath, so I didn't try. I never took time out to contemplate what had happened; I moved on. The length of the trip took so much out of me that, by the time I finished, I was just eager to put it behind me.

When I tried to write a final blog post three weeks later, I couldn't work out what to put in it. I hadn't digested the experience myself, so there was no way I could summarise the entire trip for someone else to read. I soon started receiving requests to write a book. In fact, there were far more than I expected. I'm sure most of them hoped it would be finished sooner than this, but, until 18 months after Day 174, I still had no clue what to say.

I would, therefore, like to say thank you to all those who encouraged me to write this. Whilst I hope that it has provided an interesting and sometimes amusing read, I've realised that, above all, it has given me some closure. To a large extent, I don't mind whether one person or one thousand people read this. I am just happy I have finally got my head around what was such an influential period in my life. I have tears in my eyes writing this; I've no idea why. It feels like I have just finished all over again.

BEHIND THE SCENES:
PART 2

I often say that I would not have been able to do what I did without the support of people back home. It's a massive cliché, but it is otherwise difficult to convey how much all of the encouraging comments meant to me. The truth is though, it is not completely true. Had no one else cared, I would have got by without that extra motivation. It would have been more difficult and far less enjoyable, but I would have got round. I hope that doesn't make me sound ungrateful. Every morning I was away, I would wake up and read the comments that people left on various corners of social media. It often made my day when I read a supportive or amusing comment. I am so thankful for all the recognition, but I pride myself on the fact that I would have kept the pedals turning without it.

That is not the case with the support my parents provided. They are the two people that I truly could not have done it without. I would have got nowhere without them. My idea would have remained a fantasy, and, assuming I did somehow make it to the start line on my own, I would have crumbled on the second day. Without a doubt.

My mum was often told by her friends that she shouldn't let me do this. I've heard her respond that she didn't have a choice, that my mind was made up. And it's true; I was set in my ways and I would have been devastated if she had prevented me going. However, regardless of how adamant I was, not once did she try to dissuade me. Whilst I'm sure most parents would eventually have reluctantly offered support, mine never showed a hint of doubt. I can't imagine the strength that took, and it's something that I will be forever grateful for.

I am not a very good public speaker (not at the time of writing this, anyway), and giving speeches is one thing I actively avoid doing. However, whilst crossing North America and approaching my final weeks, I decided I should say something when I finished in London, even if it was just to family that came to welcome me home. But I never did. It crossed my mind briefly at the time, but I was overwhelmed by the cameras and the number of people that showed up, so the timing never felt right.

When I made the plan to speak at the finish, I also began to plan a speech. I practised saying it a lot of times to myself when I was alone in the empty American miles. Even on my own I became emotional when reciting it. I never got round to saying it. Instead, I wrote it down and used much of it in my final blog post. I never did the words justice, but here they are in any case:

I just want to say thank you to everyone who has offered support, encouragement and/or congratulations at any point; it means the world to me. Also to everyone who came to welcome me home yesterday. It really meant a lot to see so many of you, and I apologise if I didn't get to speak to you.

One other thing – for all those that are congratulating me; at the end of the day, all I've done is turn the pedals. The amount of work done by my parents behind the scenes has been phenomenal. This trip would never have been more than an idea without them, and if it had, I wouldn't have made it past the second day. It's impossible for me to convey how much they have done in a blog, but they deserve as much, if not more, credit than I do.

I can't remember everything I had planned to say, but what I wrote in the blog covered the gist of it. I hope by now you get the idea. The whole trip was down to them. They made my plan a reality and stood by me every step of the way. I am often asked what kept me going in the harder moments. The answer is my parents. They are incredible.

COMING OF AGE

There is a bit of a cliché when it comes to backpackers 'finding themselves'. I am sure many of you are familiar with the concept of teenagers jetting off to an exotic part of Asia or South America for their gap year. They end up surrounded by loads of other people doing exactly the same thing, grow their hair long, have a marijuana-induced epiphany and come back talking a load of bollocks about how much they've grown up. Personally, I have never met anyone who has hit the stereotype quite to this extent, but you get the idea.

I have had many jokes made at my expense on this subject (probably deserved) since I have returned. I normally laugh it off and claim that I haven't changed at all, but, truthfully, I'm not sure that is the case. I do not know whether anyone else saw a change in me; frankly, I don't mind either way. There were, however, a couple of moments where I began to see myself differently.

I am fully aware that I am perilously close to sounding like a pretentious idiot (if I haven't already fallen foul of this), but I'll proceed nonetheless. The baptism of fire that was Europe battered me mentally and physically. With my knee pains, the food poisoning and the weather, I was reduced to an emotional wreck by the end of it. I emerged much stronger though, and the two days in Istanbul were enough to recover and to get back in the zone mentally. By the end of India, I felt like a champion. That country also threw its fair share of problems at me, but I felt as if I came out on top. I finished feeling tired but reinvigorated. Europe I had survived; India I had beaten.

After coming closer than I would have liked to permanent health consequences in Burma, I got through Southeast Asia fairly quickly. I struggled to grasp the fact that I had effectively cycled to Australia (minus the large, but dodgy, section that is the Middle East).

Australia was a new continent and a new challenge. I was supposedly back in Western civilisation, but I found myself riding through miles and miles of nothing. With that, came many hours of empty space and only myself for company. After spending days shouting at the wind and going slightly insane, I finished crossing the Nullarbor, and two days later I hit 9,000 miles. Halfway round the world, I felt a tangible shift in my mentality.

Three weeks later, I finished my penultimate day in Australia, and that is when it really hit home. I had spent the previous five days riding over the Great Dividing Range, and, upon cresting the final mountain, I felt a sense of unparalleled achievement. With only a leisurely 50 miles to do the following day, I had essentially completed my Australian leg. It was that evening, when I looked myself in the mirror, that I felt totally content. I still had thousands more miles to ride, lots of shit moments to endure and lots of effort to put in, but that was the first time that I *knew* I was capable of finishing what I had set out to do. Up to that point, I had been lying to myself. I kept telling myself I could do it, without fully believing it. Then it changed, as if someone had flicked a switch. I believed in myself.

With that came a startling realisation. Despite the food poisoning, the mood swings and the knee pain, there was nothing else I would rather be doing. I had set out on an assumption that I wanted to push my limits; until the end of Australia, I feared I might have made the wrong decision. I felt an immense sense of (arguably misplaced) pride, but, more than that, self-assurance. I was exactly where I was supposed to be.

MY FINAL ANSWER

That question again: why did I cycle around the world? Now that you have read my story, are you still wondering? If you are, then I am afraid to say that I don't think you will ever understand the answer. I have mentioned a few times that I did not find the trip enjoyable. That is not entirely true. It all depends on what 'enjoyable' really means to you. I would not describe what I did as fun, nor easy, nor something that I would want to do again, but I took a huge amount of satisfaction and therefore joy from it. George Mallory – a British adventurer – puts it better than I can. When asked by a *New York Times* reporter in 1923 why he wanted to climb Mount Everest, he replied:

"Because it's there."

He later elaborated when he wrote:

"People ask me, 'What is the use of climbing Mount Everest?' and my answer must at once be, 'It is of no use'. There is not the slightest prospect of any gain whatsoever. [But] if you cannot understand that there is something in

man which responds to the challenge of this mountain and goes out to meet it, that the struggle is the struggle of life itself, upward and forever upward, then you won't see why we go. What we get from this adventure is just sheer joy. And joy is, after all, the end of life."

I can't put into words what made me want to do this, because, in all honesty, I still do not know. All I know is that it is the best decision I have ever made. The instant I finished, all the pain, all the stress, all the emotions that had pushed me to the edge over the previous six months vanished. In that single moment, it all became worth it. That is the reason why.

ACKNOWLEDGEMENTS

Both the trip and this book would have been significantly different – and not in a good way – had it not been for quite a few people. There are so many that have played a part in the process and I am grateful to every one of them. I'm sorry if I miss anyone, please don't hold it against me.

First and foremost, I'd like to thank everybody who donated to the charities I rode for. I have deliberately avoided making it a constant theme in this book, but both the charities and I are incredibly grateful to all of you. All three are still fantastic causes and would still love any additional support.

Everyone else, in no particular order:
- Everybody listed in the Thank You chapter and anywhere else in this book (that goes without saying).
- Rob Thomas, Peter Watts and Pomi-T, for sponsoring me.
- Athlete Lab, for helping me get fit before the trip.
- Condor, for providing an amazing bike and amazing service.

- Showers Pass, for providing amazing gear and amazing service.
- All the guys in Strictly CC, who've been letting me ride with them since I started cycling.
- Bence Bujaki, for giving me a few much-needed bike maintenance tips before I left.
- Simon France, for giving me lots of advice about what kit/equipment I might need.
- Everybody involved in my homecoming.
- My university housemates, who put up with me spending so much time shut in my room writing this book.
- My parents. Amongst numerous other reasons, they were the first and most significant editors of my writing. It's a good thing they were around to veto a few things, otherwise this read could have been very different.
- Gail Parnell, who offered helpful insights during the editing phase of this book.
- Sue Morony, who put a huge amount of time and effort into the editing process – her advice was invaluable.
- Harry Martin, who was one of the final proof readers.
- Hannah Rummery, for all the maps and illustrations in this book. (If you're in need of a graphic designer, drop her a line: hannah@hannahrummery.com)
- James Spackman, for giving me a lot of advice in relation to publishing this book.
- Lucia Mizzoni and Peter Schmidt, for buying me the book *Tools of Titans* by Tim Ferriss as a gift. That book gave me renewed motivation, and I don't know if I would have finished my own book without it.
- Everybody who commented or liked anything on any form of social media. However insignificant all that may seem, in this situation, it really helped.

- Lindsay Corten, and everyone at Matador Publishing for making this book a reality.
- All of you reading. Thank you for buying my book (hopefully it's bought not stolen), thank you for being patient enough to make it to the end and thank you for recommending it to all your friends (*wink wink*).